Praise for
"Strategic Organizational Learning"

"*Strategic Organizational Learning* introduces a sound approach for organizational learning. At last, and long overdue, a complex subject made simple. It's a first-rate introduction for the neophyte, and an excellent comprehensive course for the most experienced executive."

Keith Grant, Ph.D.
GM University
General Motors Corp.

"Michael offers easy-to-read, critical guidance to maximize organizational learning and knowledge. He leads the reader through leading-edge research and a plethora of real-world advice. It's a must read for both scholars and practitioners."

Nido R. Qubein
President, High Point University
Chairman, Great Harvest Bread Co.

"*Strategic Organizational Learning* shows how many of the practices associated with individual learning can be linked and strategically focused to benefit the organization. This book is a must-have practical reference guide for your professional growth."

Cynthia D. McCauley, Ph.D.
Senior Fellow
Center for Creative Leadership

"Mike Beitler's work strikes a perfect balance of theory and practice; both solid research and practical models. Practitioners will appreciate the straightforward, detailed guidance on how to implement effective learning models in their organizations. It's both refreshing and encouraging to read Mike's blend of scholarly discipline and practical application."

Chris Bennett, Manager
Blue University
Blue Cross/Blue Shield of North Carolina

"Practical! Direct! Knowledge delivered in a concise straightforward manner. *Strategic Organizational Learning* slices through the fog and gets down to the brass tacks of these cutting-edge concepts. Rarely have I seen so few pages deliver such clear and profound methods for providing sustainable competitive advantage."

Richard A. Rorrer
Global Automotive Division
Tyco Electronics

"Organizational learning has become a fundamental element in striving towards optimal business management in the post-modern era, yet few organizations adequately navigate this difficult terrain. Michael Beitler's comprehensive book will demystify this challenge."

Michael J. Arena, Ph.D.
Director of Organizational Effectiveness
Ingersoll-Rand Corporation

"Beitler's text brilliantly clarifies the decisions a company must make to capture learning and link it to business strategy. One wonders upon what mishmash of concepts modern organizations built their Knowledge Management and Learning programs before '*Strategic Organizational Learning*' existed."

George Smart, CEO
Strategic Development, Inc.

"*Strategic Organizational Learning* is an extraordinary practitioner guidebook that covers all of the emerging issues in organizational learning and knowledge management. Every practitioner should own this book."

Lisa G. Withers
Training & Performance Consultant

Strategic Organizational Learning

*A **Practitioner's** Guide for Managers and Consultants*

Michael A. Beitler, Ph.D.

Copyright © 2005 Michael A. Beitler

All rights reserved. No part of this book may be reproduced, stored in a retrieval system, or transmitted, in any form or by any means, electronic, mechanical, photocopying, recording, or otherwise without the prior written permission of the copyright holder.

PRACTITIONER PRESS INTERNATIONAL

Send inquires and orders for this book to:

P.O. Box 38353
Greensboro, NC 27438

www.mikebeitler.com
or
www.amazon.com

Library of Congress Control Number 2004195687
   1. Management
   2. Organizational Effectiveness
   3. Consulting

ISBN 0-9726064-1-6

Printed in the United States of America

*I dedicate this book
to my wife,
Danyang Peng*

Acknowledgments

I owe a special thanks to my three children: to David Beitler for his technical assistance in the production of this book, and for the maintenance of my website; to Stephen Beitler for his creative design guidance on my website and printed materials; and to Rebecca Jens for her encouragement and ongoing support of my writing.

I also want to thank my many students, clients, and colleagues who have taught me so much over the years. In particular, I want to thank my following friends and colleagues:

Prof. Shelly Balbirer
Prof. Dr. Karl-Heinz Beissner
Ms. Lenora Billings-Harris, CSP
Mr. Phil Bowers
Prof. Holly Buttner
Dipl.-Kfm. Markus Faller
Ms. Nancy Ford
Ms. Carla Fox
Mr. D. Allen Frady
Ms. Jan Gilchrist
Prof. Lucy Guglielmino
Prof. Paul Guglielmino
Ms. Laura Hamilton, CSP
Dipl. Kfm. Stephan Hoersch
Herr Karl-Rainer und
   Frau Brigitte Hoersch
Dr. Catherine Holderness
Prof. Ronald Hunady
Mr. Bob Janet
Mr. Dale Jeanes
Prof. Dr. Alfred Kieser
Ms. Louise Korver
Dr. Michael Knaus
Prof. Huey B. Long

Prof. Kevin Lowe
Dr. Janis McFaul
Dr. Arlise McKinney
Mr. Ken McLeod
Mr. Chris McSwain
Dr. Lars Mitlacher
Prof. Paul M. Muchinsky
Prof. Dr. Walter Oechsler
Dr. Rick Peper
Dr. Thomas Peuntner
Prof. Dr. Gerhard Raab
Dr. Lars Reichmann
Mr. Richard Rorrer
Dr. Edith Rueger
Herr Guenther und
   Frau Hertha Rueger
Dr. Rick Shenkus
Mr. Doug Smart, CSP
Ms. Gayle Smart
Ms. Barbara Thomas
Prof. William Tullar
Dr. Mary Pat Wylie
Dipl.-Kfm. Viktor Weber, MBA
Prof. Daniel Winkler

Brief Table of Contents

I. Foundations of Organizational Learning
    1. Strategic Learning
    2. Motivation, Learning, & Development

II. Organizational Learning in the 21st Century
    3. Traditional Training
    4. Self-Directed Learning & Learning Agreements
    5. Knowledge Capture & Transfer
    6. Management & Professional Development
    7. Expatriate Training & Support
    8. Corporate Universities
    9. Consulting Skills
    10. The Future of Organizational Learning

APPENDICES
    Annotated Bibliography
    Comprehensive Reference List
    Glossary
    Subject Index
    Name Index
    About the Author

Detailed Table of Contents

PART I. FOUNDATIONS OF ORGANIZATIONAL LEARNING

CHAPTER 1 — Strategic Learning 1
From Training to Organizational Learning (OL) 2
Purpose of This Book 3
OL Practitioners 3
Practice Log 1.1 — My History With Change Efforts ... 4
Strategic Learning 5
Growing Need for OL Consultants 6
References 6

CHAPTER 2 — Motivation, Learning & Development 7
Motivational Theories 8
    Maslow & Alderfer 8
    Behavioral Theory & Motivation 9
    Cognitive Theory & Motivation 11
    Beitler's Motivation Model 11
    Self-Confidence & Motivation 13
Adult Learning Theories 13
    Behaviorists vs. Cognitivists 14
    Implications of the Two Approaches 14
    Assimilation & Accommodation 15
    Social Learning Theory 15
    Pedagogy vs. Andragogy 16
Adult Development Theories 17
    Trait Models 17

Stage Models 18
Interactional Models. 19
Summary 20
References 20

PART II. ORGANIZATIONAL LEARNING IN THE 21ST CENTURY

CHAPTER 3 — *Traditional Training* 23
Phase I: Assessing 23
Organizational Analysis 25
Job Analysis 25
Person Analysis. 27
The Goal of Assessing (NA). 27
Phase II: Designing 28
Facilitation of Learning & Transfer 30
Training Methods. 32
Phase III: Conducting 35
Lecture w/Discussion 35
Games & Simulations. 38
On-the-Job Training (OJT) 40
Phase IV: Evaluating 40
Summary 43
References 44

CHAPTER 4 — *Self-Directed Learning & Learning Agreements*. . 45
Self-Directed Learning 45
Malcolm Knowles. 46
Long & the Guglielminos. 46
Tools to Determine Appropriate Use of SDL. . . . 48
SDL in the Workplace 51
Using Both SDL & Teacher-Directed Learning. . . 51

Learning Agreements................................52
    Capture of Individual Learning 52
    Steps in Writing a Learning Agreement.........53
Using SDL & Learning Agreements 54
    Promoting Individual Learning 54
    Rewarding Individual Learning 55
    Capturing Individual Learning.................56
    Practice Log 4.1 — Who benefited?.............57
    Benefiting from Individual Learning 58
Summary...59
References..59

CHAPTER 5 — *Knowledge Capture & Transfer* 63

Codification vs. Personalization..................63
    Codification Systems 64
    Limitations of Codification Systems...........65
    Personalization Systems 66
    Practice Log 5.1 — The Open Source Community ..67
    Straddling....................................68
    Determining the Primary KM Strategy 69
    Rewards 69
Communities of Practice 70
    Origins of the Concept........................70
    The Value of CPs..............................71
    The Structure of CPs..........................72
    Cultivating CPs 74
    The Community Coordinator 76
    Life Stages of CPs 76
Summary...77
References..77

CHAPTER 6 — *Management & Professional Development* 79

Assessment 80
    In-House vs. External Assessment 81
    Assessment Instruments 81
Development 85
    Coaching/Mentoring 85
    Behavior Modeling 85
    Experiential/Sensitivity Training 86
    Job Rotation 86
    Cross-Cultural Training 87
    Career Planning 87
Performance Management 87
    Goal Setting and Performance Appraisal 88
    Rewards and Guidance Counseling 89
Succession Planning 90
    Aligning with the Strategic Plan 91
    Identifying Key Positions 92
    Identifying Candidates 92
    Real-Time Learning 93
    Line Ownership 94
    Integrating with Other Activities 95
Summary 95
References 95

CHAPTER 7 — *Expatriate Training & Support* 97

High Failure Rates 97
    The Cost of the Problem 98
The Four-Phase Training Model 99
    Self-Awareness 99
    General Awareness of Cultural Differences 100

      Specific Knowledge Acquisition 101
      Specific Skills Training 101
The Beitler & Frady Model 102
      Assessment 102
      Individualized Learning Agreements 102
      Pre-Departure Training/Orientation 103
      E-Support During Foreign Assignment 103
      Periodic Re-Assessment 103
      Learning Agreement Revisions 103
      Ongoing E-Support 104
      Who's Involved 104
      The Role of Technology 104
Cross-Cultural Design Issues 104
      Capabilities & Readiness 105
      Oechsler's Research 105
Hofstede's Research 106
Trompenaars' Work 108
      Universalism versus Particularism 108
      Individualism versus Communitarianism 109
      Neutral versus Emotional 109
      Specific versus Diffuse 109
      Achievement versus Ascription 110
      Attitudes toward Time 110
      Attitudes toward Nature & Human Nature 111
Implications for Cross-Cultural Design 111
References 113

CHAPTER 8 — *Corporate Universities* 115
The CU Model 115
      Meister's Ten Goals & Principles 117

Designing a CU......................................117
    Meister's Design Guidance....................118
    Designing the CLO Position...................119
Developing External Learning Partnerships..........120
    Partnering with Independent Vendors..........120
    Partnering with Value Chain Members..........121
Partnering with Traditional Universities............122
    Best of Both Worlds.........................122
    Customized Programs........................123
    The Multi-Company Consortium...............124
Possible Structures and Scope......................125
    Trilogy's Boot Camp.........................125
References.......................................127

CHAPTER 9 — *Consulting Skills*..........................*129*
Process Consulting................................129
    Three Consulting Approaches.................130
    The Psychodynamics of Helping...............131
    All the Things You Don't Know...............132
    Active Inquiry..............................133
    Face Work.................................134
    Summary of Process Consulting...............135
Performance Consulting............................135
    The Practice Model..........................136
    Partnering Phase............................137
    Assessing Phase.............................138
    Implementing Phase.........................138
    Measuring Phase............................139
    Summary of Performance Consulting...........141
Other Consulting Skills............................141

Appreciative Inquiry 141
Ellis's Model of Perception 142
References 143

CHAPTER 10 — The Future of Organizational Learning 145
Twelve Bold Predictions 145
ASTD's 2004 Competency Study 147
Competencies 147
Areas of Expertise 147
Roles 148
Raymond Noe's Predictions 149
ASTD's 60th Birthday 149
Some Final Predictions 150
References 151

Appendices *153*
Annotated Bibliography 153
Comprehensive Reference List 161
Glossary 173
Subject Index 185
Name Index 193
About the Author 195

CHAPTER 1

Strategic Learning

The cost of training in North American companies exceeds $60 billion per year (Blanchard & Thacker, 2004, p.4). That's an estimate of direct costs in North America. The estimates approach a quarter of a trillion dollars ($250,000,000,000) when indirect costs and opportunity costs are considered worldwide.

Understandably, senior executives are concerned about the ROI (return on investment) on these massive investments. Many executives are not convinced that the benefits of training exceed the costs. Even professional trainers themselves acknowledge "the results achieved from training, in its traditional sense, are unsatisfactory" (Robinson & Robinson, 1998, p.4).

The traditional "order-taker" trainer will not survive in the 21st century. An order-taker trainer follows this practice model:

1. wait for the phone to ring
2. take an order for a workshop (for example, a workshop on the topic of communication)
3. pull the "canned" workshop off the shelf
4. schedule a time and place for delivery
5. deliver the same old "dog-and-pony show" as promised

Clearly, this is not an appropriate or effective model for strategic partnering with senior management because this model completely ignores the unique needs of the organization.

In recent years, I have spent a considerable amount of time helping internal consultants (in-house professionals) develop more perceived value for their organizational roles. I have been teaching these in-house professionals, including trainers, consulting skills such as process consulting, performance consulting, and active inquiry.

The need to develop consulting skills will continue to grow. Trainers, as well as other in-house professionals, must grow beyond order-takers to internal consultants with high perceived value in strategic decision making. The traditional trainer must evolve into an organizational learning and performance consultant or risk being outsourced.

From Training to Organizational Learning (OL)

The field of organizational learning has evolved from "training men" (the term used in the 1940s) toward a profession of organizational learning and performance consultants. The ASTD (American Society for Training & Development), with its 70,000 members, has evolved as well. The terminology in ASTD's mission statement has changed from training to training and development, to human resource development, to workplace learning and performance.

The creation of the ISPI (International Society for Performance Improvement) has encouraged practitioners to reconsider their contribution to organizational performance. The consideration of performance issues has led to valuable discussion about how to become strategic business partners.

Traditional trainers who have focused on developing "platform skills" to make training "fun" are now having a hard time finding work. Corporations are no longer interested in trainers leading "happy sessions."

Corporations are now looking for organizational learning (OL) experts who can serve as partners in strategic decision making. Yes, OL consultants may still do some training in workshop settings. But today, OL consultants are called upon to serve senior management in organization-wide attempts to improve performance and effectiveness.

Today, OL consultants are expected to have expertise in adult learning theory, methods to promote self-directed learning, usage of learning and development agreements, knowledge capture, knowledge transfer, management and professional development, expatriate training and support, corporate universities, consulting services, and what I call "strategic learning." Don't be overwhelmed by the previous sentence. We will cover all of these topics in this book.

Purpose of This Book

The purpose of this book is to provide practitioners and executives with an overview of the emerging practices in the field of organizational learning. The material covered in this book is critical for both practitioners and executives.

I am a practitioner writing to other practitioners: *independent consultants* (OL consultants and trainers) who work for a fee, *in-house consultants* (OL consultants and trainers) who work for a salary, and students (future OL consultants and trainers).

I am also writing to executives who allocate large amounts of organizational resources to OL and training. Before becoming an OL consultant and trainer myself, I was a buyer of consulting and training.

In my work as a senior executive, I was willing to spend large amounts of money to get the advice we needed to make strategic decisions about organizational learning and performance. Unfortunately, it was difficult to find OL consultants who could assist us in strategic decision making.

OL Practitioners

Organizational learning (OL) practitioners specialize in developing "learning organizations." OL takes a big-picture approach to learning and change. OL practitioners hope to create and maintain an atmosphere that fosters continuous acquisition and dissemination of knowledge throughout the organization. Virtually all businesses today, not just high-tech companies, must be continuously learning (and changing) to stay competitive.

The literature on organizational learning speaks of individuals learning new KSAs (knowledge, skills, and attitudes) *for the benefit of the organization*. For the organization to benefit, the new learning must be "captured" and made available to all of the organization's members (Beitler, 2000).

PRACTICE LOG 1.1 — *My History with Change Efforts*

I started my career with an international management consulting firm. As a CPA, I was initially assigned to auditing and accounting engagements. While I clearly saw the importance of this work, I did not find it to be very fulfilling. I didn't feel that I was making an impact on the organization's future effectiveness.

Eventually, I had the opportunity to work in the firm's MAS (management advisory services) practice with a variety of client groups of different sizes in different industries. I found this big-picture work to be much more interesting. Developing strategic plans and reorganizing the structures of entire organizations were quite exciting.

Eventually, however, I began to question the effectiveness of these grandiose plans. Was anything really improving? Clearly, there was little change in the financial statements. In many cases, the financial statements actually looked worse. In fact, the only changes I saw in many client organizations were increases in employee complaints about management and longings for the "good ole days." Was there a problem with the MAS approach? What about the people issues?

After several years of practicing the MAS approach at the management consulting firm, I spent ten years as a senior vice president in banking. During this time, I was responsible for the training and development programs. We developed "good" programs, but it was difficult to see the contribution to the organization's bottomline.

Finally, after many years of frustration as both consultant/facilitator and manager/leader of learning and change efforts, I developed a systematic, strategy-driven approach to organizational learning. I want to share that approach with you in this book.

Strategic Learning

The first step for the OL consultant is to be sure the organization has a well-crafted strategic plan that clearly communicates how senior management intends to fulfill the organization's mission. Frequently, the organization has a vague mission and/or an unrealistic strategic plan. In such cases, the OL consultant should recommend a strategic planning session with the senior management team.

Only after the organization has a well-crafted, well-communicated strategic plan, can the OL consultant determine if the current organizational structure, culture, and human processes will support the organization's strategy. Invariably, attempts to implement even the best-crafted strategy will fail, if the organization's structure, culture, and human processes are not supportive.

In my book entitled *Strategic Organizational Change* (Beitler, 2003), I offered the following model, called "Targets for Change."

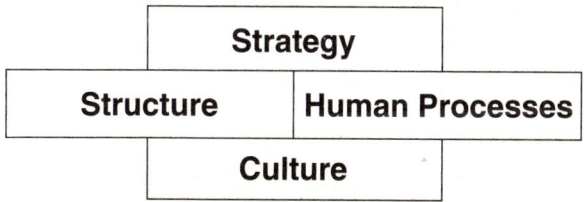

FIGURE 1.1 Targets for Change

In that book, I discussed a step-by-step process in which organizational change (OC) consultants could diagnose four different types of organizational problems (or opportunities). Then I offered a variety of alternative interventions for each type of diagnosed problem (or opportunity).

Since writing that book, I have frequently been asked, "What type of organizational change is organizational learning?" Organizational learning problems (and opportunities) require a combination of human process changes and organizational culture changes. Like any other organizational change efforts, organizational learning activities and programs (interventions) need to be driven by the organization's strategic plan.

"Strategic learning" is learning that is focused on helping the organization fulfill its strategic plan.

Growing Need for OL Consultants

As the world we live in becomes more and more competitive, the need for OL consultants to facilitate organizational learning will continue to grow. Senior management must depend on OL consultants to maximize the organization's investment of money, time, and other resources to build its human capital into a sustainable competitive advantage.

OL consultants must become experts in the use of traditional training, self-directed learning, learning agreements, knowledge capture and transfer, management and professional development, expatriate training and support, corporate universities, and general consulting skills. The future looks bright for this new breed of professional.

This book will provide an overview of emerging practice in organizational learning. This book will serve as a reference book for both practitioners and executives.

Let's begin by looking in Chapter 2 at the foundational theories and concepts that support successful OL practice. Novices as well as experienced practitioners should find this to be a helpful review.

REFERENCES

Beitler, M.A. (2000). Contract learning in organizational learning and management development. In H.B. Long & Associates (Eds.), *Practice and theory in self-directed learning*. Schaumberg, IL: Motorola University Press.

Beitler, M.A. (2003). *Strategic Organizational Change*. Greensboro, NC: Practitioner Press International.

Blanchard, P.N. & Thacker, J.W. (2004). *Effective training* (2nd ed.). Upper Saddle River, NJ: Pearson/Prentice Hall.

Robinson, D.G. & Robinson, J.C. (1998). A focus on performance: What is it? In D. Robinson & J. Robinson (Eds.), *Moving from training to performance*. Alexandria, VA: ASTD, and San Francisco: Berrett-Koehler.

Chapter 2
Motivation, Learning, & Development

All of us are theorists. We develop theories to explain how the world works. Yet the mere mention of the word "theory" leaves my clients and students cold.

The reason for this aversion to theory is rooted, I believe, in our experience with classroom instruction focused on theory divorced from practical application. Kurt Lewin insisted on the marriage of theory and practice. Lewin is well-known for saying, "There is nothing more practical than a good theory."

This chapter (more so than any other chapter in this book) will contain a lot of theory, but it is practical theory. In this chapter, you will find only theory with practical applications for organizations attempting to acquire, capture, and transfer learning.

Ultimately, our goal is to improve performance at the individual, group, and organizational levels. Performance is made up of multiple factors. Throughout this book, we will refer to the following performance formula:

Performance = KSAs + Motivation + Environment

FIGURE 2.1 The Performance Formula

KSAs are the knowledge, skills, and attitudes required to perform a job well. Training is a possible solution for KSA deficiencies. But as the performance formula indicates, training is *not* the answer for all performance problems. Training will not solve motivation-related or environment-related performance problems.

Motivation-related performance problems include factors such as poorly designed reward systems. Environment-related performance problems include excessive interruptions, old equipment, poor raw material quality, bottlenecks in production, communication breakdowns, and poor working conditions. Clearly, training will not solve any of these problems.

When diagnosing performance problems, it is important to make a distinction between training (KSA) needs and non-training (motivational or environmental) needs. A needs analysis should reveal deficiencies in KSAs, motivational factors, and/or environmental factors. Any motivational or environmental needs revealed in the needs analysis should be discussed with the managers who have the authority (and motivation) to make the necessary changes. We will look at how to do a needs analysis in the next chapter.

Motivational Theories

For many of you, this section will be a basic review of the motivational theories you learned in a "Principles of Psychology" or an "Organizational Behavior" course. It is essential that you are familiar with these theories as they provide a basis (along with adult learning theory, which we'll discuss next), for effective use of the strategies and techniques covered later in this book.

Maslow & Alderfer

Let's begin with Maslow's (1954) Hierarchy of Needs model. Many academics refuse to accept this as a scientific model, but practitioners (managers and consultants) use it every day. The model is simple, but the implications for practice are powerful.

Maslow believed there were five levels of needs; the lower level needs must be satisfied before the higher level needs become motivating. Maslow envisioned needs in the following hierarchy:

Practically speaking, most of the organizational members we are working with are not focused on their physiological and safety needs; they are focused on higher-level needs. Since few people are operating at the self-actualization (SA) level, most people we'll encounter are focused on their social and esteem needs. To motivate these individuals, we must show them how their efforts will fulfill their social and esteem needs.

FIGURE 2.2 Maslow's Hierarchy of Needs

Alderfer's (1969) ERG theory builds upon Maslow's theory. Alderfer's existence needs correspond with Maslow's physiological and safety needs. Alderfer's relatedness needs correspond to Maslow's social needs. And Alderfer's growth needs correspond to Maslow's esteem and self-actualization needs.

Keep in mind, it is our unsatisfied needs that motivate us. Satisfied needs are no longer motivating. Appealing to somebody's satisfied needs will not lead to motivation.

Alderfer's theory recognizes more complexity in the motivation process than did Maslow's. Alderfer spoke of needs that expand over time, such as a desire for better food or a bigger house.

Behavioral Theory & Motivation

In a spirit of full disclosure, I must admit I don't like behavioralism or the behaviorists (e.g., Watson and Skinner). I believe behavioralism dehumanizes people by ignoring their wonderful cognitive abilities. In graduate school, I had the opportunity to take a course with Albert Ellis, the leading cognitive psychologist, so I confess to being an advocate of cognitive psychology.

However, in a spirit of fairness, I must admit that the behaviorists have made some valuable contributions to our understanding of motivation. John Watson said, "Whatever behavior you reward, you get more of." The implication for all of us (not just trainers and managers) is clear; we must design and maintain reward systems that encourage desired behaviors. A poorly designed, or maintained, reward system that rewards the wrong behaviors can render an otherwise well-designed training or learning program ineffective.

The behaviorists spoke of positive reinforcement, negative reinforcement, and punishment. Understanding these three concepts is essential in designing a reward system.

Positive reinforcement involves the receipt of something desirable after a behavior. Negative reinforcement is the removal of something undesirable (a double negative). Both positive reinforcement and negative reinforcement are positive events. Both are valuable in management and training because both encourage (motivate) positive future behaviors.

Punishment should not be confused with negative reinforcement. Punishment does not encourage positive future behavior; its purpose is to eliminate negative future behaviors. While punishment is sometimes appropriate (e.g., firing an employee for theft or poor customer service), it must be used sparingly.

The inappropriate use of punishment can lead to several problems:

1. It does not motivate people to do the right thing. Instead, people become focused on not doing the wrong thing; it can lead to doing nothing, in order to remain "safe."
2. It establishes somebody (e.g., manager or trainer) as the "punisher." Punishers are not well liked; punishers are feared. Punishers are not in a position to build positive working relationships. Nobody wants to build a relationship with the punisher.
3. It requires constant monitoring. If the wrong behavior still offers some kind of reward, some individuals will continue the wrong behavior when the punisher is out of sight.

Cognitive Theory & Motivation

Cognitive psychologists, including Albert Ellis, reject the S-R (stimulus-response) model of the behavioral psychologists as too simplistic (Ellis & Dryden, 1987). Ellis offers the following A-B-C model to help us understand the role of perception:

A   Activating Event
B   Belief about the Activating Event
C   Consequential Behavior or Thinking

The "A" (activating event) in Ellis's model corresponds to the "S" (stimulus) in the behavioral model. The "C" (consequential behavior or thinking) corresponds to the "R" (response) in the S-R model.

Ellis suggests that the "B" (belief about the activating event) is what causes the subsequent behavior (or thinking). The "B" is the result of our cognitive processes. These cognitive processes are what separate us from animals.

As managers, trainers, or consultants we must understand somebody's belief about an activating event (the "B"), if we hope to understand his or her behavior. These beliefs (perceptions) are a combination of expectations, values, and assumptions. Only through skillful questioning can we understand what is motivating somebody else's behavior or thinking.

Beitler's Motivation Model

My own motivation model is based on Victor Vroom's (1964) Expectancy Theory. Vroom's model is widely accepted in the academic world because of its complexity. Unfortunately, it is ignored by practitioners for the same reason.

My own model of motivation (considerably simpler than Vroom's) is meant to be used as a tool in practice. My model takes the form of a simple mathematical equation:

$$\begin{array}{c}\text{Level} \\ \text{of} \\ \text{Motivation}\end{array} = \begin{array}{c}\text{Expectation} \\ \text{of} \\ \text{Success}\end{array} \times \begin{array}{c}\text{Trust in} \\ \text{Receiving} \\ \text{the Reward}\end{array} \times \begin{array}{c}\text{Perceived} \\ \text{Value of} \\ \text{the Reward}\end{array}$$

FIGURE 2.3 Beitler's Motivation Model

Whenever someone (manager or trainer) tries to motivate someone else (subordinate or trainee), all three factors must be considered. Let's use the example of a manager trying to motivate a subordinate. The manager says, "If you successfully complete this task you will be rewarded with _____."

Immediately, the subordinate considers his or her expectation of success. If the expectation of successfully completing the task is low, motivation will be low.

If the subordinate's trust in receiving the reward is low, motivation is low. Perhaps other employees have been promised a promotion or bonus for completing the same task, but they did not receive a promotion or bonus.

Finally, the subordinate will consider his or her perceived value of the reward. Once again, if the perceived value of the reward is low, motivation will be low.

As you know, whenever you are doing multiplication, if any of the factors are zero, the result is zero. The implications are significant.

If the subordinate believes that the possibility of successfully completing the task is zero, no amount of money (or perceived value of a reward) will motivate him or her. If the subordinate's trust in receiving the promised reward is zero, no amount of money (or perceived value of a reward) will motivate him or her.

Finally, if the value of the reward is perceived as zero, motivation is zero unless the subordinate is motivated by something other than the promised reward. Please note, what matters here is the subordinate's perception, not the manager's.

This model of motivation suggests how critically important the open and honest communication of expectations and values is to organizational effectiveness.

Self-Confidence & Motivation

What is often mistakenly called a motivational problem can be a self-confidence problem. Albert Bandura has made some valuable contributions to the concept of self-efficacy. Self-efficacy is defined as one's feelings about one's own competency.

Bandura (1977a) stated that individuals with low self-efficacy are preoccupied with concerns about failure. Ford, Smith, Weissbein, Gully, and Salas (1998) added to Bandura's insights with their research. They found, in various situations, that individuals with high self-efficacy try harder; those with low self-efficacy often reduce their effort or give up.

Blanchard and Thacker (2004) added a valuable insight by saying, "If failure is expected, the employee acts to minimize the negative consequences of failure. For example, withdrawing from the activity (refusing to try) moves the person away from proven failure to simply 'I didn't try!'" (p. 84).

Building self-confidence is often a necessary "pre-learning" activity. A lack of self-confidence should be revealed during a needs analysis.

ADULT LEARNING THEORIES

Everybody claims to have experienced learning, yet nobody seems able to clearly define what learning is. We know that learning occurs physically. "Learning is related to changes in the physical, neuronal structure of the brain and its related electrochemical functioning" (Blanchard & Thacker, 2004, p.85). Unfortunately, debating definitions of learning and discussing brain activity during learning are beyond the scope of this book.

For our purposes, we need to be aware of the two opposing approaches to learning theory and the implications of those approaches for adult and organizational learning. The two different approaches, behavioral and cognitive, have the same roots as those discussed in the previous section on motivation.

Behaviorists vs. Cognitivists

Behaviorists define learning as a relatively permanent change in behavior. The behaviorists de-emphasize the brain or mental activity in the learning process. B.F. Skinner (1971), the most ardent of behaviorists, believed the brain is simply like any other organ; its neural activities are conditioned to occur based upon a past history of consequences. "Learning occurs when new consequences are experienced" (Blanchard & Thacker, 2004, p. 86).

Cognitivists define learning as a change in cognition. Cognition refers to the mental processing of information. Cognitivists believe, "Even though learning can be inferred from behavior, it is separate from the behavior itself" (Blanchard & Thacker, 2004, p.85). As in the previous section on motivation, I agree with the cognitive theorists.

Implications of the Two Approaches

As you can imagine, there are significant differences in practice when training or learning is designed and conducted by a behaviorist, as opposed to a cognitivist. Let's look at a few of the implications:

	Behavioral	**Cognitive**
Instructional Goals	Trainer Developed	Collaboratively Developed
Learner's Role	Passive	Active
Trainer's Role	Director	Facilitator
Control	Trainer	Learner

FIGURE 2.4 Practice Implications of the Two Approaches

The implications are quite dramatic. "In the behaviorist approach, the trainer controls learning by controlling the stimuli and consequences that the learner experiences" (Blanchard & Thacker, 2004, p.86). In the cognitive approach, it is assumed learners have their own goals, priorities, and learning style preferences.

The behaviorist approach has obvious applications for childhood education, but I question its use in adult education and training.

Assimilation & Accommodation

Piaget is best known for his work on child development, but his insights are also valuable for adult and organizational learning.

Piaget (1954) spoke of "assimilation" and "accommodation" in terms of cognitive maps. Cognitive maps are made up of categories created to help us understand the world.

When we experience something for which we have an existing category we can assimilate it into that category. When we experience something for which we do not have an existing category we must accommodate for it by creating a new category.

During my college days, I took a calculus course. The instructor, a brilliant engineer, assumed we could assimilate the new information (calculus) into our cognitive maps of the world. Unfortunately, while he could assimilate calculus into his existing categories containing engineering tools, none of us in the class had such categories. What we needed was help in creating a new category to accommodate for this new knowledge.

We must remember that people need ways to organize their experiences (and knowledge) to enable them to understand the world around them. We can help facilitate the assimilation and accommodation processes.

Social Learning Theory

Bandura's (1977b) "Social Learning Theory" proposes that individuals can learn by observing others and the consequences of other people's behavior. Since this learning comes through observing others, Bandura's theory is also called observational or vicarious learning. But there is more to Bandura's theory than the learning power of observation.

Bandura also stressed the importance of "attention" and "retention." He believed the learning process does not begin until the learner's attention is focused. There are serious implications here for trainers. Objectives and benefits for the learner must be discussed first to obtain learner attention. Put simply, no attention, no learning.

Adults do not retain all the information they see or hear. Bandura believes trainers can facilitate the cognitive process of retention. There are many ways available. Noe (2005) states, "Behaviors or skills can be coded as visual images (symbols) or verbal statements" (p.110). Blanchard and Thacker (2004) add, "This process, cognitive organization, can be facilitated in training by asking the trainees to provide examples of how the new information relates to what they already know" (p.99).

Pedagogy vs. Andragogy

Malcolm Knowles (1990) made a major contribution to our understanding of adult learners by giving us the concept of "andragogy." Until Knowles, pedagogy, the study of teaching children, dominated learning theory. "Pedagogy gives the instructor major responsibility for making decisions about learning content, method, and evaluation" (Noe, 2005, p.114). Pedagogy clearly applies to teaching children; it is generally ineffective when teaching adults.

Knowles' theory of andragogy makes the following five assumptions about adult learners:

1. they need to know why they are learning something
2. they need to be self-directed
3. they bring work-related experiences with them
4. they have a problem-solving approach to learning
5. they are motivated by both extrinsic and intrinsic rewards

Clearly, adult learners are seeking a facilitator for their learning projects, not an all-knowing guru. Adult learners want to retain as much control as possible over the learning process.

Knowles's theory of andragogy leads us into a necessary, albeit brief, discussion of adult development theories.

Adult Development Theories

Understanding adult development theories sheds much light onto adult learning needs. The theories of adult development can be classified into three basic categories:

1) trait models — in which patterns of individual behavior are seen as being constant over time (exemplified by Allport's theory),

2) stage models — in which development is seen as predictable changes over time (exemplified by the theories of Erikson and Levinson),

3) interactional models — in which development is seen as the result of the interaction among age-related, cohort/history related, and non-normative life events (exemplified by the work of Neugarten and Schlossberg).

Trait Models

Supporters of the trait (or stability) models of adult development use trait theory to support their beliefs. Trait theorists believe traits (e.g., friendliness or aggression) account for the consistency in human behavior. The leading trait theorist, Gordon Allport (1897–1967), suggested, "If a person's traits are known, it is possible to predict how he or she will respond to various environmental stimuli" (1937, p.28). In other words, "traits will guide their behavior, because people can respond to the world only in terms of their traits" (Hergenhahn, 1990, p.182).

Allport believed people react differently to the same stimulus because different traits are involved. While Allport believed each individual was unique because of his or her unique combinations of traits, he believed that traits were basically fixed. Allport is well-known for his following statement about the fixed nature of human traits: "The same fire that melts the butter hardens the egg" (1961, p.72). The influence of environmental factors is determined by one's nature.

Stage Models

Numerous theorists (Piaget, Freud, Erikson, and Levinson) have argued for stage (or predictable change) models of development.

Erik Erikson (1902-1990) was once a follower of Freud. An important contribution of his theory is the epigenetic principle. According to Erikson (1980), the concept of epigenesis has its roots in the biological principle that development of an embryo proceeds according to a predetermined plan. With this plan, each organ has its own time of maximum growth and development. If the parts develop properly, they will eventually form an integrated, functional whole. In psychosocial terms, Erikson translated the epigenetic principle to say that the demands of one stage lay the groundwork for the resolution of future tasks.

Erikson is best known in developmental psychology for his model of eight stages of development. His sixth and seventh stages, concerning young and middle adulthood, provide a foundation for the current stage models of adult development.

In 1978, Daniel Levinson, a social psychologist at Yale University, published his book entitled *Seasons of a Man's Life*. The book greatly expanded Erikson's seventh stage of adult development (generativity vs. stagnation), but emphasized the crisis nature of the midlife stage.

Levinson (1978) sees human development not as a continuous process, but as alternating stages of stability and change. This concept of alternating periods of stability and instability is clearly Piagetian. Levinson's concept of the life cycle suggests an underlying pattern to human growth similar to Erikson's epigenetic principle. Levinson believes that individuals proceed in an age-related series of emotional and physical transitions.

Some stage theorists (Gould, 1978; Levinson, 1978) believe the midlife transition is the great transition. The focus of this stage is on the loss of youth and faltering physical powers that had been taken for granted. Additionally, there is a yearning for "individualness" and "undividedness." No matter what a person is doing or has done, parts of him/herself have been suppressed. The major task of this stage is the reintegration of the ignored parts.

The stage theorists assure us that a period of stability will follow the turbulent midlife transition. Like Freud's stage theory, they see adults moving into and out of midlife transition like clockwork—unfinished business or not. In other words, midlife transition is just a stage (like the "terrible-two's"); adults grow out of it.

Interactional Models

Advocates of the interactional (or flexible-contextual) models, argue that the first two types of models are too simplistic. While most two-year-olds are at a similar developmental level (and exhibit similar behaviors), a forty-year-old professional athlete has little in common with a forty-year-old heart surgeon.

Historically, Carl Jung was one of the first writers to offer a model of midlife development that was not based on assumptions of predictability. While Jung believed fundamental changes in adult development occurred at about age forty, he "understood individual adult development as a product of both psychological processes and cultural forces" (Miesel, 1991, p.52).

Bernice Neugarten and other researchers at the University of Chicago "point out that their studies show that chronological age is an increasingly unreliable indicator of what people will be like at various points in their development" (Miesel, 1991, p.60). Neugarten went on to say, "The scenarios and schedules of our lives are so varied that it is virtually impossible to talk about a single timetable for adult development" (Miesel, 1991, p.60).

Nancy Schlossberg (1987) says her research indicates that chronological age is one of the least important factors in the differences between how people experience transitions. Schlossberg says, "because the adult years are so variable, we cannot assume that particular transitions will necessarily occur at specific ages" (p.75). She believes what determines the positive or negative effects of the transition are how the individual views the transition, and his or her resources for dealing with it.

The supporters of interactional models argue that what was true for Levinson's (1978) group (a particular cohort) will not necessarily be true for another cohort born into a time with different economic and social challenges. Interactional models are built upon the interactionist belief that the individual affects, and is affected by, his or her environment.

Summary

An understanding of the motivation, learning, and development theories covered in this chapter is critical to successfully applying the strategies and techniques discussed in this book. For a deeper understanding of any of these theories, read some of the referenced materials at the end of this chapter.

Now let's shift our focus from theory to practice.

REFERENCES

Alderfer, C. (1969). An empirical test of a new theory of human needs. *Organizational Behavior and Human Performance*, 4(2), 142–75.

Allport, G.W. (1937). *Personality: A psychological interpretation*. New York: Holt, Rinehart, & Winston.

Allport, G.W. (1961). *Patterns and growth in personality*. New York: Holt, Rinehart, & Winston.

Bandura, A. (1977a). Self-efficacy: Toward a unifying theory of behavioral change. *Psychological Review*, 84: 191–215.

Bandura, A. (1977b). *Social learning theory*. Upper Saddle River, NJ: Prentice Hall.

Blanchard, P.N. & Thacker, J.W. (2004). *Effective training: Systems, strategies, and practices* (2nd ed.). Upper Saddle River, NJ: Pearson/Prentice Hall.

Ellis, A. & Dryden, W. (1987). *The practice of rational-emotive therapy*. New York: Springer Publishing.

Erikson, E. (1980). *Identity and the life cycle*. New York: Norton.

Ford, J., Smith, E., Weissbein, D., Gully, S., & Salas, E. (1998). Relationships of goal orientation, metacognitive activity, and practice strategies with learning outcomes and transfer. *Journal of Applied Psychology*, 83: 218–33.

Gould, R. (1978). *Transformations: Growth and change in adult life*. New York: Simon & Schuster.

Hergenhahn, B.R. (1990). *Theories of personality* (3rd ed.). Englewood Cliffs, NJ: Prentice Hall.

Knowles, M.S. (1990). *The adult learner* (4th ed.). Houston: Gulf Publishing.

Levinson, D. (1978). *The seasons of a man's life*. New York: Alfred A. Knopf.

Maslow, A.H. (1954). *Motivation and personality*. New York: Harper & Row.

Miesel, J.A. (1991). *A phenomenological exploration of the experience of voluntarily changing one's career during midlife*. Unpublished doctoral dissertation. The Union Institute, Cincinnati, OH.

Noe, R.A. (2005). *Employee training and development* (3rd ed.). New York: McGraw-Hill Irwin.

Piaget, J. (1954). *The construction of reality in the child*. New York: Basic Books.

Schlossberg, N. (1987). Taking the mystery out of age. *Psychology Today*, 21(5), pp.74–85.

Skinner, B.F. (1971). *Beyond freedom and dignity*. New York: Bantam/Vintage.

Vroom, V. (1964). *Work and motivation*. New York: Wiley.

CHAPTER 3

Traditional Training

It may seem strange to start the second part of this book, entitled *Organizational Learning in the 21st Century*, with a chapter on traditional training. Authorities agree that traditional, trainer-driven, classroom training will continue to diminish in importance as a delivery method for organizational learning. Traditional training, which has historically been the recipient of billions of corporate dollars, will be allocated a decreasing percentage of the organization's budget.

Even the ASTD (American Society for Training & Development) has changed its mission from training to workplace learning and performance. Many trainers (both in-house and independent) now believe they must become performance improvement consultants to continue to be valuable to their clients. I'll have more to say later about this evolution from trainers to performance consultants.

So, if traditional training is decreasing in importance, why should we study it? Simply because traditional training practice and theory still shape how many executives (and trainers) think about learning in organizations. Understanding traditional training practice and theory will provide the historical perspective that is necessary to appreciate the exciting emerging issues that will dominate organizational learning practice in the twenty-first century.

In this chapter, we will look at the four phases of traditional training: assessing, designing, conducting, and evaluating.

PHASE I: ASSESSING

Everyone agrees that the first phase of training is assessing. But many trainers still refer to this phase as "training needs analysis"

(TNA). This term disturbs me because TNA presupposes that there is a training need.

The organization's leaders are concerned about performance problems. They are interested in training only as a possible way to fix performance problems.

All performance problems cannot be fixed with training. Many performance problems have non-training roots. Non-training problems, in the form of motivation problems or environmental problems (e.g., logistics, raw materials) cannot be fixed with training.

Remember the Performance Formula in Chapter 2:

Performance = KSAs + Motivation + Environment

Figure 3.1 The Performance Formula

While I do not bother to correct trainers or clients who use the term "training needs analysis" (TNA), I prefer the term "needs analysis." Needs analysis (NA) recognizes that the assessing phase will reveal both training needs (KSAs) and non-training needs (motivational and environmental). It's critical to make this distinction.

The goal of training is to improve performance. Since we are hoping for improved performance at the individual level, the job level, and the organizational level, our assessment must include data gathering and diagnosis at all three levels.

Assuming we find training needs, the goal of the assessing phase (NA) is training *objectives*. These objectives will become the criteria for designing, conducting, and evaluating the training. NA should determine two things: 1) the required KSAs (knowledge, skills, and attitudes) of the job, and 2) the current KSA levels of the trainee.

There is another important benefit of NA. By conducting interviews, surveys (questionnaires), and observations with job incumbents and supervisors, we enhance "buy-in" for the training.

Getting the support, or buy-in, from line managers is essential for effective training design and for effective training transfer (after the training session is completed).

Organizational Analysis

The first of the three levels of assessment (NA) is the organizational-level analysis. Effective training *must* be aligned with, and supportive of, the organization's strategic plan. If the strategic plan is non-existent, unclear, or obviously inappropriate, the OL consultant or training designer should recommend a strategic planning meeting (see Beitler 2003, Chapter 7).

The organizational analysis begins with reading the organization's mission statement for insight into the leadership's vision of how the organization fits into the external environment. The external (environmental) analysis includes, but is not limited to, customers, suppliers, competitors, and regulators. The mission of the organization should be the leaders' vision for the organization's purpose in its larger environment.

An internal analysis of the organization should look at the organization's structure, culture, reward system, resources, policies, procedures, work design, and workflow. These organizational elements must be in alignment with the organization's strategic plan and supportive of the training and development efforts.

The strategic plan is management's commitment to a process of fulfilling the organization's mission. The strategic plan provides the priorities needed to design training and development programs. For example, the choice of a low-cost leader strategy (as opposed to an innovation leader or any other generic strategy) should significantly affect the training and development programs of the organization.

Job Analysis

Job analysis involves the examination of the KSAs required by a particular job.

> ### Practice Log 3.1 Focusing on the Relevant
> While most authors discuss organizational analysis before job analysis, I have found it is essential *in practice* to have a particular job(s) in mind before beginning organizational analysis. There is a mind-boggling amount of data available at the organizational level. It is important to focus only on data that is relevant to the particular task at hand.

In job analysis (for training purposes), we want to identify roadblocks that can keep employees from doing an effective job. In NA we will uncover both training needs and non-training needs.

If performance problems are due to low levels of current KSAs (compared to the required KSAs of the job), training can increase performance. But if performance problems are due to low motivation or an unsupportive environment (both of which are non-training needs), training will *not* increase performance.

In job analysis, we want to know what the job entails. What KSAs are required to be successful in the job?

An important question is "who to ask?" Who can share insight about the job being analyzed? Two obvious candidates are the incumbent (the person currently doing the job) and the supervisor. Here are a few tips for dealing with incumbents:

1. use a cross-section based on tenure,
2. get a wide range of input (it increases "buy-in"),
3. interview in small groups (for "piggy-backing" insights),
4. select the incumbents yourself.

After you gather the insights from the supervisor, look for discrepancies compared to the incumbents' comments. Don't be surprised if you discover communication problems. Differences in expectations, due to poor communication, are fairly typical.

What if there are no incumbents? What if the job is new? You can contact the manufacturer of the equipment used on the job and/or speak with people in similar jobs or positions in other companies.

Try to identify specific expectations for successful job performance. These include specific knowledge expectations, skills expectations, and attitude expectations.

Person Analysis

Person analysis involves the collection and analysis of data about the person's current levels of KSAs. If the organization has a formal performance appraisal process, that is a good place to start. Supervisor appraisals typically include expectations for the job and the employee's current success in fulfilling those expectations. Be aware that political/interpersonal issues, or a poor appraisal instrument, can distort the picture of the employee's job performance.

Many companies now use 360-degree performance appraisals. These can provide additional insights from peers, subordinates, and maybe even customers. Don't underestimate the importance of the self-ratings. Discrepancies between the supervisor and the employee can lead to fruitful discussions about job expectations.

When doing person analysis for attitude training and/or management development it is important to use the well-researched, validity-tested preference instruments that are currently available. Some of the most helpful preference instruments are the Myers-Briggs Type Indicator, the FIRO Element B, and the Campbell Interest and Skills Survey. If you are not licensed or qualified to buy, administer, and interpret these instruments, work with a colleague who is.

The Goal of Assessing (NA)

NA should produce clear objectives for the training or development program. NA should make a clear distinction between training needs and non-training needs. In addition to this distinction, the NA may reveal that the problem is the design of the job itself.

Redesigning the job may be easier and more effective than designing additional training (see Beitler 2003, Chapter 8).

One last thought should be considered in NA: it should be reactive and proactive. The reactive approach focuses on the current KSA needs of the employee. The proactive approach focuses on the future KSA needs of the employee. Consider both!

PHASE II: DESIGNING

After we have completed a thorough NA, we should have clearly defined objectives for the training or development program. Clearly defined, well-written objectives have the following three components:

1. desired outcomes — What should be expected from the trainee after the training? (able to count, list, solve, install, replace, sort, recite at a specific level of competence),

2. conditions — Under what conditions should the desired outcomes be expected to occur? (in a training session, in real-life, or in an emergency situation, for example),

3. criteria for success — What criteria will be used to determine successful outcomes? (standards for accuracy, quality, speed, judgment).

Written objectives should be understandable by the average person. If the objectives are not easily understood, they should be re-written.

I should point out that the objectives for attitude training (the "A" of KSAs) are a little different from the objectives in knowledge and skills training (the "K" and "S"). The objective in attitude training is to provide trainees with information that contradicts inappropriate attitudes.

Typically, it is unproductive to directly attack negative attitudes. That approach simply results in more defensiveness.

For example, an attitude-training workshop about teamwork would be designed around the objective: "to increase the workers' awareness of the positive aspects of teamwork."

Well-written training objectives benefit the person in each of the following roles: (Of course, one individual could play more than one of these roles.)

1. trainee — his or her stress level is reduced because the expectations are clear,
2. training designer — he or she has guidance for designing an appropriate program,
3. training purchaser (someone assigned the task of purchasing training from an outside vendor) — he or she will have guidance to evaluate competing vendors,
4. trainer — he or she will know what points to emphasize and will be able to judge the progress of the trainees (for in-progress adjustments),
5. training evaluator — he or she can use the objectives to compare actual outcomes with desired outcomes.

A major consideration in training design is organizational constraints. One constraint is limited resources. No organization has unlimited resources. The following important questions are sometimes frustrating, and sometimes political, but always crucial:

1. What resources are available?
2. Who will receive the training?
3. What type of training is appropriate in the organization?
4. What's the strategic plan and mission of the organization?

Trainees themselves can act as constraints on certain training options. Two subgroups, with dramatically different KSA levels, may require two different training programs. Wide variations in training readiness may require the development of self-paced modules, instead of sessions involving all of the trainees simultaneously. Other options might include several small groups of trainees or individualized learning agreements.

Before discussing training methods and their appropriateness, let's take a look at some facilitation issues.

Facilitation of Learning & Transfer

In the training design phase, we must consider several facilitation issues concerning learning and transfer of learning. These issues should be uncovered during the NA. These issues include learning-style preferences, motivation, emotional baggage, and goal setting.

We know from extensive research that trainees have different learning-style preferences (such as visual vs. auditory). These preferences should be considered in training design.

Motivation and expectation levels should also be revealed during the NA. We know that trainees with high motivation and expectation levels learn more. To improve motivation and expectations, we should design the following elements into the program:

1. show trainees they have the ability to succeed (learn),
2. show trainees the positive outcomes,
3. show trainees the value of the training for them personally.

Emotional baggage must be eliminated or managed, if effective learning is to take place. Previous negative experiences and their negative consequences should be discussed to reduce trainee anxiety. High levels of anxiety can make it difficult for trainees to focus on the training material.

Specific goals will direct the trainees' efforts. Providing intermediate goals and feedback will help the trainees reach the ultimate learning goals of the program.

Attention, retention, and transfer are three critical design issues. Let's take a brief look at each one.

No learning occurs until attention has been established (Bandura, 1977). Trainees will focus on what's important to them. Explanation of the benefits to the trainees should be designed into the program. Distractions should be reduced or eliminated (such as uncomfortable chairs, posters, noise, and hot or cold room temperatures).

Retention is enhanced by using prior learning and by helping the trainees with cognitive reorganization. By connecting the new information to the trainees' existing knowledge, retention is improved. Stimulating recall, by asking the trainees to reflect on their previous experiences, should be designed into every program. Cognitive reorganization is the process of re-arranging the information into a logical system for future use. The trainer should facilitate this process.

Transfer of training has been an important discussion in the training literature for many years. Training that cannot be transferred back to the job is considered of little value by corporate executives. Relevant training material must be properly designed to enhance transfer. Design issues here include:

1. massed vs. spaced practice,
2. whole vs. part training,
3. overlearning,
4. maximizing similarity vs. varying the situation.

Massed practice is appropriate for difficult and complex tasks. Four straight hours (as opposed to four one-hour sessions) with brief follow-up sessions would enhance transfer for difficult, complex tasks. Spaced practice is appropriate for general knowledge.

The appropriateness of whole or part training is determined by the nature of the skill being learned. Some processes, such as the accounting cycle, can be divided into logical steps: 1. record journal entries, 2. post to the general ledger, 3. take a trial balance, for example, and then taught in a step-by-step manner.

"Overlearning" should be designed into the program when trainees will use what they have learned in emergency situations. Overlearning is simply the continuous practice of a skill even after successful performance is demonstrated. "Automaticity" should be the objective of training designed for police SWAT teams and other emergency/crisis workers. (As opposed to "compilation," which is appropriate in situations where there will be time to refer to a manual or notes before acting.)

Training Methods

There are many training methods/techniques available to training designers. Every method has strengths and weaknesses. No single method is always appropriate.

For our purposes, we will limit our discussion to three general types:

1. lecture w/discussion

2. games and simulations

3. on-the-job (OJT)

Lecture w/discussion is important to training designers because virtually all training involves some lecture and some discussion. Lectures and discussions should not be seen as either/or, but as a continuum:

All Lecture   All Discussion

Appropriate uses for all lecture or all discussion are rare. We should think in terms of percentage of lecture usage combined with percentage of discussion usage. The best use of lecture is with large numbers of people, limited time, and a training need for declarative knowledge (factual information).

Straight lecture (all lecture) has some limitations. Few trainers are stimulating lecturers; straight lectures are usually boring for trainees. Research shows trainee attention declines after 15 or 20 minutes, and it does not pick up again until the trainer says "and my final point is _____."

Adding discussion can improve on the inherent weaknesses of lectures. When the trainer asks questions, he or she stimulates trainee thinking, even if the trainees don't verbally respond. Asking questions can keep the trainees focused. Feedback from the trainees can help guide the trainer's presentation.

There are several other considerations when using discussion. Discussion shifts control to the trainees. Discussion re-shapes the program content. It allows for the particular interests of the trainees to emerge, resulting in increased training relevance.

The strengths and weaknesses of lecture and discussion must be considered in the design of every training and development program.

Games and simulations are designed to demonstrate various processes, and a large number of these are available. We will look at only a few here: equipment simulators, business games, the in-basket technique, case studies, role playing, and behavior modeling.

Equipment simulators can be very expensive (such as flight simulators). In some cases, such as pilot training, the expense is justified. But equipment simulators can also be done with equipment that is simply pulled out of production for a few hours (such as cash registers or widget-making machines). When using equipment simulators, it is important to design in the psychological conditions encountered on the job.

Business games demonstrate real-world tasks encountered in a particular industry, company, or department. They enhance higher-level learning by stimulating systemic thinking. Business games allow trainees to see the results of their decisions. Trainees can compete against each other or compete against a computer.

The in-basket technique provides trainees with training on items typically found in the in-basket of the job incumbent. The trainees must prioritize and respond to each memo, message, or report. Trainees should receive feedback on their responses from the trainer.

Case studies are ideal for strategic knowledge training. Written or videotaped cases provide the history, key elements, problems, and opportunities of a real or imagined company. Trainees diagnose and arrive at solutions for the company individually or in groups. The goal here is the understanding of the advantages and disadvantages of various solutions. With cases about real companies, the trainees can be asked to go to the internet to update the case's information.

Role playing is appropriate for people-skills training. Even observers in role-play exercises gain new insights. By rotating the "actors," various points of view are understood.

Behavior modeling, also for people-skills training, involves an expert (possibly the trainer) demonstrating the correct way to do something. Ideally, the trainees will have an opportunity to attempt to duplicate the expert's performance (videotaping is beneficial here). Feedback should be provided to the trainees.

Games and simulations provide a safe place for learning. A prerequisite for their success is a sufficient level of declarative knowledge (gained through earlier lectures or experience).

On-the-job training (OJT) is the most frequently used type of training in organizations. It simply involves more-experienced workers training less-experienced workers. OJT is generally seen as cheap and informal.

However, OJT is typically not cheap because there is an opportunity cost involved in taking experienced workers away from their positions. OJT also involves the cost of waste and breakage that occur during training. Effective OJT should also include "train-the-trainer" costs.

There are several important advantages of OJT:

1. the problem of low transfer of new KSAs from the training room to the job site is eliminated,
2. it provides new-employee orientation to company culture and procedures,
3. it enhances relationship development between experienced and new employees.

OJT should be formalized for maximum effectiveness. The following steps should be followed:

1. preparation — break the job down into essential skills, and then design appropriate training,
2. presentation — tell, demonstrate, explain
3. learner demonstration — a) trainee "talk-through," b) trainee attempts the task, c) trainer feedback, and d) trainee practice,
4. periodic follow-up

PHASE III: CONDUCTING

I have told students for many years that the easiest phase of training is the conducting phase (the actual delivery of the workshop). Many students erroneously believe that acquiring platform skills is difficult, but that, once acquired, these skills are sufficient to convert any individual into a dynamic and effective trainer. In fact, the conducting phase (and the use of platform skills) is quite simple, if you have done a good job with the assessing and designing phases.

Acquiring platform skills or "tricks of the trade" is relatively quick and easy with the help of a mentor. We will cover some of the tricks of conducting training here. In the previous section, we covered three general types of training. Let's follow the same format here:

1. lecture w/discussion
2. games and simulations
3. on-the-job training (OJT)

Lecture w/Discussion

As stated in the previous section, lecture w/discussion is typically a part of every training program, so learning how to use it effectively is important for training success.

Lecture is designed to transmit declarative knowledge (facts and information). The purpose of integrating discussion into the lecture is to allow the trainee an opportunity to "work with" the new knowledge. This approach increases both attention and retention.

While some enthusiastic groups of trainees will start and maintain exciting discussion without the trainer's prompting, it is the responsibility of the trainer to initiate and direct a productive discussion.

Effectively leading and directing discussion is based on the skill of questioning. Questioning has been used by great teachers throughout the ages. Socrates, the great ancient philosopher, led others to the truth by asking one question after another. The Socratic method is still an effective teaching tool today.

Trainers should use both closed-ended and open-ended questions. Closed-ended questions lead to specific answers. Asking "What are the four phases of a specific procedure?" will result in an answer containing the names of the four phases, but nothing more.

Open-ended questions require no specific responses. Open-ended questions sometimes result in unpredictable responses. They often lead into a discussion of a topic that is not on the agenda. Open-ended questions allow for a re-direction of the training session to topics of interest to the trainees. The trainer is relinquishing some control to the trainees. This procedure may add time to the original plan; it may also lead to questions the trainer cannot answer.

The strategies for using open-ended and closed-ended questions may appear obvious. Open-ended questions "open up" the discussion. Closed-ended questions can be used to bring a discussion back under control. Everybody has experienced classes or training sessions that have drifted off-course into unproductive chat. A closed-ended question can re-focus the discussion.

The distinction between overhead questions and direct questions is critical for conducting effective training. Overhead questions are directed at the whole group of trainees. Direct questions are used to draw responses from particular trainees.

Overhead questions are appropriate when the trainer wants all the trainees to draw upon their previous knowledge and experience.

Working adults always have valuable knowledge and experience to draw upon.

A direct question is appropriate when the trainer knows a particular trainee has specific knowledge or experience to answer a particular question. The trainee's specific knowledge or experience is a valuable resource that should be tapped. Of course, "psychological safety" for trainees is essential. The trainer should always come to the rescue of any trainee who is struggling with an answer. Be sure to provide the trainees with a safe atmosphere for learning.

Another platform skill is the effective use of relay questions and reverse questions. These questions are directed back (bounced back) to the trainees. They are an excellent way to start a new discussion because the trainer can immediately spot trainee interest.

Relay questions re-ask the question of the whole group. A reverse question re-asks the question of the individual raising the question. It's sometimes obvious to the trainer that the trainee already has an answer or opinion. The question itself thinly masks the desire to speak out on the subject. The trainer has the option of allowing the discussion to go in that direction or not.

Every trainer eventually meets a tough crowd (the group of trainees who act like clams). This tricky situation can produce very uncomfortable moments for some trainers. If the trainer asks a question and then answers it, the trainees will simply wait for the trainer to answer every future question.

The key with clams is not to speak first. The trainer must wait for a response. The first waiting period (usually during the early moments of the first training session) can be almost physically painful. But the trainer must wait or, at most, offer additional information to consider.

Another trick with highly introverted groups is to get the trainees to write down their responses. This activity gives them time to arrange their thoughts before speaking out. Discussing individual responses in small groups is a good way to reduce apprehension caused by larger groups. Obviously, all of the questioning techniques will work better if the trainer begins the training session with an icebreaker. Trainees who know each other are more likely to share their thoughts and feelings.

Let me share a few more tips or platform skills that will improve the conducting of the training phase. Moving around the room (or platform) allows the trainer to "walk off" his or her nervous energy. Being animated creates a moving visual for the trainees to watch. Plus, it makes the trainer appear confident, friendly, and enthusiastic.

During discussions, be sure to acknowledge each trainee's contribution (at least with a thank you). Remember to use nonverbal cues when others are speaking. A nod or a smile of approval encourages trainees to respond to future questions.

Be a good listener. Don't guess what the trainee is going to say. And be patient; the trainee is probably still trying to organize his or her thoughts. If you are not sure what the trainee is asking or saying, try to summarize the person's thoughts. If you are wrong, let the trainee explain further. It's worth the time!

Provide variety. Researchers tell us that attention declines after 15 or 20 minutes of lecture. Do something new after 15 or 20 minutes of lecture (ask trainees for examples, tell a story, play a game, do a group exercise, play an audio or video clip, ask trainees to write something, or take a break).

Many trainees are visual learners. Use a large number of visuals. Put an outline of key points on the chalkboard; check off the items as they are completed. Capture important points on flipchart paper, and then tape the flipchart sheets to the wall for future reference.

Games & Simulations

Games and simulations can be time consuming (and expensive). They may take up to an hour or several days. Remember, a debriefing session is necessary after every game or simulation.

Let's look at how to conduct four popular methods:

1. in-basket technique
2. case studies
3. role playing
4. behavior modeling

The in-basket technique involves putting samples of memos, phone messages, and reports from the in-basket of the training's target job. The trainee should read and respond to the items by organizing, prioritizing, and making decisions. The trainer should ask "What criteria did you use?" Feedback from the trainer is critical for the trainees. Learning is enhanced in this simulation by asking each trainee to complete a "Lessons Learned" form. This form, which simply says "Lessons Learned" at the top, forces trainees to reflect on the learning experience.

Case studies are highly effective training tools in corporate training. They allow individuals or small groups to work on applying their new knowledge to real-life situations. The chosen case must reflect the learning objectives of the training program. The trainer must deflect requests for his or her own solution by applying the Socratic questioning method that we discussed earlier.

Role playing is useful when trying to teach trainees job-related people skills. It is especially effective when conducted in triads (initiator, responder, and observer). The trainees should rotate through all three roles. The trainer should monitor the exercise; it may be necessary to stop the exercise if it gets off track. Reflection and discussion about what went wrong can be very insightful. In role playing, it is critical to demonstrate what happens when the skill is not used.

Behavior modeling involves modeling by an expert, who can be either the instructor or an expert on video. Ideally, the trainees have the opportunity to watch the expert's behavior as well as their own on videotape. Trainer feedback helps the trainees modify future behavior. This is an excellent method for learning sales and/or management skills. This type of training is most effective when it focuses on only a few points.

OJT

Effective OJT is much more costly and time-consuming than it appears. Effective OJT requires train-the-trainer sessions, incentives for trainers, and periodic evaluations of trainers. The first two training phases of assessing and designing are critical before attempting to conduct OJT. The assessment phase must include a thorough job analysis and person analysis. The design phase must consider the characteristics of the job, the trainer, and the trainees.

OJT should be formalized so senior management knows what is being trained and how.

"Facilitating" Facilities

The facilities, the training room in particular, should enhance or "facilitate" learning. Some suggestions are obvious: padded, comfortable chairs with arm rests, carpet to absorb sound, and no distracting noises. Some other suggestions are not so obvious. For example, the length of the room should not exceed the width by more than 50 percent. The farther away the trainee feels from the trainer, the farther the trainee feels from the discussion. There are also some controversial suggestions. Some training experts firmly state, "No windows." Personally, I like windows because of the warm, natural light. (Sometimes it's OK to disagree with the experts.)

PHASE IV: EVALUATING

Of the four phases of training, evaluating receives the least attention. Many trainers, both internal and external, avoid the evaluating phase. Perhaps they don't want to see their mistakes receiving attention.

But the realities of organizational life are changing in the twenty-first century. Good management now requires ongoing evaluation of all organizational activities. All organizational activities require time and money; all leaders of organizational activities must be held accountable. Senior management now demands evidence that training makes a positive contribution to the organization.

"How do we evaluate the results of training?" is a question I frequently hear. The answer is, by comparing the results to the objectives of the training. The assessing phase (NA) should have concluded with written objectives for the training. These written objectives are the basis for evaluating the actual results.

It is true that many companies still do not do training evaluation, thereby allowing ineffective training programs to continue. Proper evaluation procedures would save considerable time and money. Feedback for improvement should always be seen as a positive process.

It is a sign of integrity and professionalism when a trainer performs an objective training evaluation. I believe senior managers appreciate this strategy, especially in an ongoing relationship.

There are two types of training evaluation: process evaluation and outcome evaluation.

After a training program, process evaluation looks at data from before and during training. Before-training process evaluation assesses three components:

1. the effectiveness of NA,
2. the formulation of training objectives,
3. the designing of the training.

Process evaluation should analyze the appropriateness of instructor notes, case studies, videos, handouts, etc.

Outcome evaluation typically receives more attention from senior managers. They want to compare planned outcomes with actual outcomes (results). There are four different types of outcome data to evaluate:

1. reaction outcomes,
2. learning (KSA) outcomes,
3. job behavior outcomes,
4. organizational outcomes.

Most adults are familiar with reaction outcome data. This data is gathered from the trainees at the end of the training session. These evaluation forms are usually handed out to trainees at "five minutes before five o'clock." They don't assess learning itself; they gather trainee attitudes, opinions, perceptions, and emotions. The value of this data is based upon the assumption that favorable reactions enhance the motivation to learn. Affective questionnaires measure general feelings; utility questionnaires measure beliefs about the training's value.

Reaction questionnaires gather data concerning the following four components:

1. training relevance — "perceived" value (if the perceived relevance is low, trainers must change beliefs about the training, or change the training itself)

2. training materials and exercises — trainee reactions to books, videos, and experiential exercises

3. trainer(s) — perceptions of trainer effectiveness (entertaining, competent, friendly, or helpful)

4. facilities — noise, temperature, refreshments, furnishings.

Learning (KSA) outcome data is frequently gathered with the use of pre- and post-training instruments. Knowledge (K) outcomes typically use paper-and-pencil tests (such as stating the rules covering search and seizure procedures). Skills (S) outcome data involves before and after demonstrations. Attitude (A) outcome data compares before and after opinions.

Job behavior outcome data is important to senior management because it focuses on the transfer of learning back to the job. This outcome data is harder to gather because the trainer needs help to gather the data. The trainees' supervisor or peers must be willing to share their evaluations of the trainees before and after training.

Organizational results (outcome) data is an important notion, but it is difficult to gather in practice. Of course, senior management wants to know the training's effect on the bottom line. Unfortunately, some results are difficult (if not impossible) to quantify.

At the organizational results level, there is the problem of "confounders." Training does not happen in a vacuum. There are multiple causes for performance levels: training, technology, job design, quality of materials, logistics, for example. Improvements in some areas may cause deficiencies in others. It is virtually impossible to control all of the variables.

Senior management also wants to see an analysis of the cost of training (Is the training worth it?). Training professionals need not be cost accountants, but they should be aware of the basics. A cost/benefit analysis implies that the benefits must be greater than the costs. Development costs include the costs of TNA, design, evaluation, and results tracking. Direct costs are directly attributable to the training (can be eliminated if the training is cancelled). Indirect or overhead costs include utilities, facilities, administration, and other allocatable costs (can't be eliminated even if the training is cancelled). Such costs are expenditures that have already been made (such as the cost of the closet full of manuals). Cost accounting is not an exact science. Trainers should be prepared to argue if they are unfairly allocated indirect (overhead) costs.

Lastly, trainers should be familiar with the concepts of internal validity, external validity, and reliability. These concepts are invariably raised when somebody questions the use of an evaluation instrument or data-gathering method. While a discussion of these topics is beyond the scope of this book, a trainer must educate him/herself on these concepts before doing training evaluation.

Summary

This has been a brief overview of traditional training practice and theory. The purpose of presenting this overview is to provide a historical reference for understanding the exciting, emerging issues that will dominate organizational learning in the twenty-first century.

Let's move on to look at these emerging practices now!

REFERENCES

Bandura, A. (1977). *Social learning theory.* Upper Saddle River, NJ: Prentice Hall.

Beitler, M.A. (2003). *Strategic Organizational Change.* Greensboro, NC: Practitioner Press International.

CHAPTER 4
Self-Directed Learning & Learning Agreements

In the competitive environment of the twenty-first century, organizations can no longer depend solely on "traditional" training and development, which focuses on designing and delivering workshops for groups of people. While workshops will remain as part of an organization's OL strategy, workshops alone will not be sufficient to create a sustainable competitive advantage.

Organizations of all sizes must become "learning organizations."

A learning organization is an organization that promotes, rewards, and captures individual learning for the benefit of the organization.

(Beitler, 2003, Chapter 12)

Becoming a learning organization requires the utilization of both self-directed learning and learning agreements. In the second part of this chapter, we will look at how to use learning agreements to "capture" an individual's self-directed learning for the benefit of the organization.

Let's look first at the use of self-directed learning in a learning organization.

SELF-DIRECTED LEARNING

The literature on self-directed learning (SDL) is now growing at an exponential rate. In addition to countless articles and books, the *International Journal of Self-Directed Learning* debuted in 2004.

Over the past thirty years, an impressive body of literature has developed concerning the theory, practice, and potential of SDL. Tough (1979) speaks of *independent learning*—learning, for the most part, independent of teachers and institutions. Tough's approach to learning, with little or no institutional support, is also shared by the advocates of *distance learning* (e.g., Garrison, 1987). Knowles (1975) speaks of self-directed learning in institutional settings.

Malcolm Knowles

For our purposes, I think the best definition of SDL is that of Malcolm Knowles. He defines SDL as a process in which:

> individuals take the initiative, with or without the help of others, in diagnosing their learning needs, formulating learning goals, identifying human and material resources for learning, choosing and implementing appropriate learning strategies and evaluating learning outcomes.
>
> (Knowles, 1990)

While I found the work of Knowles to be inspiring, I had two reservations concerning the use of self-directed learning. Based on my own teaching, training, and consulting experience, I realized:

1) some intelligent adults are not psychologically equipped (or "ready") to succeed at self-directed learning, and

2) some subject matters (e.g., accounting) are not appropriate for self-directed learning.

Long & the Guglielminos

My first concern was addressed in the works of Huey B. Long, and in the extensive research of Lucy and Paul Guglielmino with the self-directed learning readiness scale (SDLRS).

Long (1989, 1990, 1991) addresses the psychological aspects of SDL. Long (1989) depicts the successful self-directed learner as having the following characteristics:

1. self-confidence,

2. self-awareness,

3. self-reflectiveness,

4. a strong goal orientation, and

5. an aptitude for systematic procedures.

Obviously, all organizational members do not exhibit these characteristics.

In his 1991 book chapter, entitled *Challenges in the Study and Practice of Self-Directed Learning,* Long presents his four-quadrant model identifying situations in which SDL is (and is not) appropriate, based on the psychological make-up of the individual (p.22). It is important to note that Long (1991) prefers to speak in terms of degrees of individual self-direction, rather than in terms of "all-or-nothing" (p.15).

Measuring "readiness" for self-directed learning is the focus of the work of Lucy and Paul Guglielmino. As part of her dissertation work in 1977 at the University of Georgia, Lucy Guglielmino developed and field tested the Self-Directed Learning Readiness Scale (SDLRS), a Likert-type questionnaire with five response options per question (Guglielmino, 1978). The SDLRS was later expanded to its current 58 items. The SDLRS has become the most widely used instrument for assessment of self-directed learning readiness (Long & Ageykum, 1988; McCune, 1989; Merriam & Brockett, 1997). The self-scorable form for the SDLRS is called the Learning Preference Assessment (Guglielmino & Guglielmino, 1991a, 1991b).

Based on a compilation of more than 3000 respondents to the instrument, the Pearson split-half reliability of the English version is .94 (McCune, Guglielmino, Garcia, 1990). Further discussion of the validation studies on the SDLRS can be found in Brockett and Hiemstra (1991), Delahaye and Smith (1995), and Guglielmino (1997).

Research has suggested that individuals who have developed high self-directed learning skills tend to perform better in jobs requiring high degrees of problem-solving ability, creativity, and change.

The average score for adults who complete the SDLRS is 214 (with a standard deviation of 25.59). The following scoring ranges have been established:

Low	58–176
Below average	177–201
Average	202–226
Above average	227–251
High	252–290

Individuals with low or below average SDLRS scores usually prefer very structured learning options, such as lectures in traditional classroom settings. Individuals with average SDLRS scores are likely to be successful in more independent situations, but are not fully comfortable with handling the entire process of identifying their learning needs, planning their learning, and then implementing their learning plan. Individuals with above average or high SDLRS scores usually prefer to determine their own learning needs, plan their learning, and then implement their learning plan. (This does not mean people with above average or high SDLRS scores never choose to be in a structured learning situation. They may choose traditional courses or workshops as a part of their learning plan.)

The adult version of the SDLRS has been translated into French, Spanish, Japanese, Chinese, Korean, German, Finnish, Greek, and Italian. The SDLRS has been used in more than 75 doctoral dissertations. For further information about the SDLRS, write to Guglielmino & Associates, 734 Marble Way, Boca Raton, FL 33432.

Tools to Determine Appropriate Use of SDL

My concern about individual readiness for SDL was addressed in the work of Long and the Guglielminos. But I was still concerned about the indiscriminant use of SDL without regard to the subject matter being learned. Certain business subjects (such as accounting), by nature, require the direction of a teacher/trainer. For example, the non-accountant does not know what he/she doesn't know, or how to go about learning it. Self-directed learning could lead to mis-education.

To guide the appropriate use of SDL based on subject matter, I created *The Continuum of Business Education* (Figure 4.1). Greater learner participation (more trainee group discussion or SDL) is appropriate as one moves to the right on the continuum.

Teacher-Directed (Training)		Learner-Directed (Development)
Technical Skills Courses	*People Skills Courses*	*Conceptual Skills Courses*
accounting finance	team building conflict management	leadership strategy

Source: Beitler, M.A. (2000).

FIGURE 4.1: The Continuum of Business Education

The Continuum of Business Education recognizes the need of organizational members to acquire three types of skills: technical, people, and conceptual. These three types of skills are quite different in nature and require different teaching/learning strategies. While lectures may be effective for accounting or finance, acquiring people skills requires the use of group discussion and role playing. Conceptual skills, different from both technical and people skills, require teaching/learning techniques that emphasize critical thinking and integrative thinking (e.g., case studies).

The Continuum of Business Education is helpful once the organizational members have demonstrated that they are ready to succeed at SDL. Lucy Guglielmino's SDLRS instrument is designed to indicate learner readiness to engage in SDL.

While the learner characteristics are addressed in the work of Long and the Guglielminos, the subject matter/environmental characteristics are addressed in depth in my own work (Beitler, 1999, 2000).

It is necessary to analyze three sets of variables to determine if SDL is appropriate. Analyzing the three variables (teacher characteristics, learner characteristics, and subject matter characteristics) is facilitated by using the following checklist:

	Teacher-Directed	Learner-Directed
1. The teacher's characteristics		
knowledge	high	low
experience	high	low
2. The learner's characteristics		
SDLRS score	low	high
knowledge	low	high
experience	low	high
maturity level	low	high
motivation level	low	high
ability to set goals	low	high
3. The subject matter/environmental characteristics		
"block of knowledge"		
—defined by profession	high	low
time availability	low	high
resource availability	low	high

FIGURE 4.2: The SDL Variables Checklist

Circling items on the left side of the Checklist indicates a need to move to the left (teacher-directed) side of the Continuum of Business Education. Circling items on the right side of the Checklist indicates a need to move to the right (learner-directed) side of the Continuum.

SDL in the Workplace

Several U.S. companies have been implementing SDL as part of their long-term OL strategies. Guglielmino and Murdick (1997) report the following companies using SDL: Motorola, Disney, Aetna, U.S. West, Levi Strauss, Owens-Corning, and American Airlines.

Several studies (Durr, 1992; Merriam, 1993; Piskurich, 1993) note a number of efficiency and effectiveness reasons for using SDL:

1. SDL has greater relevance to the particular needs of the individual learner.
2. SDL allows greater scheduling flexibility.
3. SDL promotes meta-skills for approaching and solving problems beyond the immediate learning project.
4. SDL allows for frequent and timely updating of skills and knowledge.
5. SDL can provide more focused learning in highly specialized fields.

Also, as individuals "develop their self-directed learning skills, they tend to become more self-confident and more apt to solve problems on their own" (Guglielmino & Murdick, 1997).

Using Both SDL & Teacher-Directed Learning

It is important not to think of self-directed versus teacher-directed education in terms of which one is better. There is not an ideal here; we must think in terms of which one is appropriate.

Is it possible for teacher-directed and self-directed learning to occur simultaneously in a single organization? Yes; in fact, both should be occurring simultaneously at all levels of the organization. Managing multiple teaching/learning projects throughout the organization can be facilitated by the use of learning agreements. Let's look now at the benefits individuals and organizations gain from the use of learning agreements.

LEARNING AGREEMENTS

I have been a vocal advocate for the use of learning agreements (also called learning contracts) in organizations for many years (Beitler, 1999, 2000). But I didn't invent the concept.

Contract learning was advocated throughout the 1970s and 1980s by Malcolm Knowles (1975, 1986). Knowles, who taught graduate students at Boston University and North Carolina State University, found lecturing to older students ineffective because of their unique backgrounds and needs. Knowles decided to write a learning contract with each of his students. The contract was an agreement between teacher and student; it detailed what would be learned and how it would be learned (Knowles, 1986). Knowles' concept of the learning contract has been implemented in numerous graduate schools, including Norwich University (Montpelier, Vermont) and The Union Institute (Cincinnati, Ohio). Throughout the 1990s, I advocated the use of learning agreements with mid-career professionals and managers in organizational settings (Beitler, 1999, 2000).

While I have been an advocate of *self-directed learning* in organizations (discussed in the previous section), I have always kept one of Knowles' warnings in mind. Knowles (1986) cautioned, "some people get so enamored of one technique that they use it in every situation, whether it is appropriate or not" (p.3). To heed his admonition, I try to consider every imaginable technique before determining "the best" one for a specific learner to acquire a specific skill (or knowledge).

Capture of Individual Learning

While I can argue for the use of both teacher-directed learning and self-directed learning in the organization (based on the SDL Variables Checklist), it is more important to discuss how to capture individual learning for the benefit of the entire organization. That result is one of the major advantages of learning agreements. A learning agreement between the supervisor and his/her subordinate can incorporate both teacher-directed and self-directed learning, as appropriate.

These agreements provide guidance for the supervisor and subordinate; they also provide a way to document, capture, and share knowledge throughout the organization. These agreements can provide the foundation for a learning organization in which individuals engage in self-directed study and then share their new knowledge with other organizational members (e.g., participation in group or peer discussions). These group discussions (we will look at these further in the next chapter) enhance the critical-thinking skills of the individual and add to the knowledge base of the organization.

Steps in Writing a Learning Agreement

Learning agreements are actually quite simple to write, if they are incorporated into the employee performance evaluation process. The performance evaluation should include a determination of the employee's learning and development needs.

Once the learning and development needs are agreed upon by employee and supervisor, only four writing steps are necessary (Beitler, 1999):

1. What will be learned?
2. How will it be learned?
3. How will the learning be documented?
4. How will the learning be evaluated?

The first step involves determining the learning objectives for the upcoming year. What will be learned must be determined (and agreed upon) before how it will be learned is considered.

The second step specifies the resources that will be used (for example, books, journal articles, workshops, mentoring, experiential learning).

The third step defines how the learning will be documented (for example, through thematic papers, reaction papers, annotated bibliographies, videotapes).

The fourth step defines how the learning will be evaluated, who will conduct the evaluation, and what the evaluation criteria will be.

When incorporated into the annual performance appraisal process, learning agreements do not substantially increase the workloads of individual managers and workers. Learning agreements, utilizing both self-directed learning and teacher-directed learning, can dramatically improve an organization's ability to promote, reward, capture, and benefit from individual learning.

USING SDL & LEARNING AGREEMENTS

With the use of SDL and learning agreements, the organization takes major steps towards becoming a learning organization. Remember the earlier definition?

"A learning organization is an organization that promotes, rewards, and captures individual learning for the benefit of the organization."

Now, with the concepts of self-directed learning and learning agreements in mind, let's look at how to *promote*, *reward*, and *capture* individual learning for the benefit of the organization.

Promoting Individual Learning

Nobody denies that self-directed learning takes place in organizations. Long and Morris (1995) found more than fifty articles and papers published between 1983 and 1993 concerning SDL in business and industry.

Foucher's (1995) interviews with HR practitioners revealed four organizational variables that promote SDL in the workplace:

1. the presence of a participative management style;
2. a supportive environment in which employees enjoy autonomy, and in which management believes the employees are competent and motivated;
3. support for experimentation and tolerance for error; and

4. support for unplanned, non-sequential learning activities.

Foucher's (1995) work corroborates Baskett's (1993) findings in his study of workplace learning. Baskett found the following factors important in enhancing organizational learning:

1. opportunities for employees to contribute to the organization's goals and values,
2. an environment of trust and mutual respect,
3. support for risk taking and innovation, and
4. collaboration among organization members.

One powerful way of promoting learning in general, and self-directed learning in particular, is to write learning goals into the learning agreement of every employee. If the learning goals are accomplished, the employee should be rewarded, as he or she would be for reaching any other goal.

Rewarding Individual Learning

Organizational reward systems should reinforce desired behaviors —those behaviors that support the organization's strategic plan and mission. The behavioral psychologists tell us, *Whatever behavior you reward, you get more of.* Managers must be careful about what activities they reward.

Every organization should be concerned about performance management. Performance management systems include goal setting, performance appraisal, and rewards (reinforcements for desired behaviors). As stated earlier, the learning agreement should clearly set learning goals for the individual. The annual (or semi-annual) performance appraisal should compare learning goals with actual learning accomplished. If the goals in the previous learning agreement have been met, they should be rewarded.

When using learning agreements, goal setting should be a collaborative process. If employees are involved in the goal-setting process, they are more likely to buy-in. Goals energize and focus behavior.

The goal-setting process should begin with a learning needs analysis. The goals in the organization's strategic plan should be considered first, followed by the goals of the department or group. The goals determined for the individual should be both personally satisfying and supportive of the organization's strategic plan.

Performance appraisals are essential because they provide a feedback loop for employees. Generally speaking, most employees are trying to do a good job, but they need guidance. Performance appraisals should be seen as the critical link between goal setting and rewards.

Organizations should, at minimum, consider using a 360-degree feedback system, in which employees receive performance appraisal feedback from supervisors, peers, and subordinates. More feedback data leads to more insight. Once again, feedback should be elicited on behaviors that are significant to implementing the organization's strategic plan.

The rewards themselves can be either extrinsic or intrinsic. Traditionally, organizations have relied heavily on extrinsic rewards (particularly money). But ultimately, the overuse of cash rewards will weaken the company's competitive position.

Intrinsic rewards can, in many cases, be more motivating than extrinsic rewards. Intrinsic rewards involve the satisfaction derived from the work itself. Intrinsic rewards can be highly motivating in the learning process. If the employee is studying something interesting or beneficial for career advancement, he or she will be quite enthusiastic. So, clearly we want buy-in during the goal-setting process.

Capturing Individual Learning

Capturing individual learning is a necessity for converting individual learning into organizational learning.

The third step in writing the learning agreement involves how the learning will be documented. These documents (for example, thematic papers, reaction papers, annotated bibliographies, videotapes), once created, should be made readily available to organizational members. These documents can be posted on the company's intranet or in one of the more sophisticated electronic knowledge management systems that are now available. Of course, the old-fashioned methods still work too: file cabinets, memos, and hard-copy reports.

Capturing learning experiences eliminates a large amount of duplicated effort. For example, if one employee finds a particular workshop to be a waste of time, the organization wants to be sure not to send anybody else. It is important is to capture these experiences.

We will look at the capture and transfer of knowledge in more detail in the next chapter.

Practice Log 4.1 — Who benefited?

When I was working in banking, our bank president approved my verbal request to attend a one-week workshop in New York City. All expenses (tuition, books, airfare, hotel, meals, and taxi fares) were paid—no strings attached.

As I was flying home after the workshop, I was looking over my notes and thinking about telling Bob (one of our senior managers) about some of the great ideas that were shared during the workshop. Bob had been wrestling with some of these issues for months.

On my first day back on the job, I saw Bob running down the hallway toward me. I could hardly wait to tell him about what I had learned. Bob saw me and said, "Mike, long time, no see. Have you been sick?"

"No," I quickly responded, "I've been at a workshop in New York."

Bob looked at his watch and said, "Glad to hear you are feeling better," then ran down the hallway.

Would you believe that nobody, not a single person, ever asked me about that workshop? Who benefited?

Organizations must promote individual learning, but organizations will not benefit from it unless the individual learning is captured and made available to organizational members. At a minimum, reaction papers (positive or negative) from organizational members who have attended workshops should be reviewed before an organization commits to sending more participants to the same workshop.

Benefiting from Individual Learning

The literature on organizational learning speaks of individuals learning new KSAs (knowledge, skills, and attitudes) for the benefit of the organization. It is important to analyze the learning needs of both the individual and the organization. Confessore and Kops (1998) state, "the learning organization must account for the learning needs of both the individual and the organization" (p.371).

The new individual KSAs must then be collected and transformed into organizational learning. Confessore and Kops (1998) believe, "all the perspectives used to describe organizational learning include some dimension of transforming individual knowledge into collective knowledge—that is, knowledge determined, shared, interpreted, and used collectively throughout the organization" (p.366). Dixon (1994) defined organizational learning as a process by which information (determined by the organization as meaningful) is communicated by and throughout the organization. Other writers, including Senge (1990), emphasized the importance of a systemic approach to learning in the organization.

Watkins and Marsick (1993) defined six imperatives for an organization to benefit from learning in the workplace:

1. creating continuous learning opportunities,
2. promoting inquiry and dialogue,
3. encouraging collaboration and team learning,
4. establishing systems to capture and share learning,
5. empowering people to have a collective vision, and
6. connecting the organization to the environment.

Summary

The concept of the learning organization, while inspiring, will remain only a concept without the use of SDL and learning agreements.

An organizational culture in which continuous learning occurs at every level of the organization should be the goal and definition of the learning organization.

REFERENCES

Baskett, Morris (1993). *Workplace factors that enhance self-directed learning.* (Text No. 93-01-002). Montreal, Canada: Group for Interdisciplinary research on Autonomy and Training, University of Quebec at Montreal.

Beitler, Michael A. (1999). Learning and development agreements with mid-career professionals. *Performance in Practice*, Fall 1999. American Society for Training & Development.

Beitler, Michael A. (2000). Contract learning in organizational learning and management development. In H.B. Long and Associates (Eds.), *Practice and theory in self-directed learning.* Schaumburg, IL: Motorola University Press.

Beitler, Michael A. (2003). *Strategic organizational change.* Greensboro, NC: Practitioner Press International.

Brockett, R. & Hiemstra, R. (1991). *Self-direction in adult learning: Perspectives on theory, research, and practice.* London: Routledge.

Confessore, Sharon J. & Kops, William, J. (1998). Self-directed learning and the learning organization: Examining the connection between the individual and the learning environment. *Human Resource Development Quarterly*, 9(4), pp. 365–375.

Delahaye, B.L. & Smith, H.E. (1995). The validity of the Learning Preference Assessment. *Adult Education Quarterly*, 45(3), pp.159–173.

Dixon, N.M. (1994). Organizational learning: A review of the literature with implications for HRD professionals. *Human Resource Development Quarterly*, 3(1), pp. 29–49.

Durr, Richard E. (1992). An examination of readiness for self-directed learning and selected personnel variables at a large Midwestern electronics development and manufacturing corporation. (Doctoral dissertation, Florida Atlantic University.) *Dissertation Abstracts International*, A 53/06, p. 1825.

Foucher, Roland (1995). *Enhancing self-directed learning in the workplace: A model and a research agenda.* (Text No. 95-01-005). Montreal, Canada: Group for

Interdisciplinary Research on Autonomy and Training, University of Quebec at Montreal.

Garrison, D.R. (1987). Self-directed and distance learning: Facilitating self-directed learning beyond the institutional setting. *International Journal of Lifelong Education*, 6(4), pp. 309–318.

Guglielmino, Lucy M. (1978). Development of the Self-Directed Learning Readiness Scale (Doctoral dissertation, University of Georgia, 1977). *Dissertation Abstracts International*, 1978, 38, 6467A.

Guglielmino, Lucy M. (1997). Reliability and validity of the Self-Directed Learning Readiness Scale and the Learning Preference Assessment. In H.B. Long & Associates, *Expanding horizons in self-directed learning* (pp. 209–222). Norman, OK: College of Education, University of Oklahoma.

Guglielmino, Lucy M. & Guglielmino, Paul J. (1991a). Expanding your readiness for self-directed learning: *A workbook for the Learning Preference Assessment*. King of Prussia, PA: Organization Design and Development.

Guglielmino, Lucy M. & Guglielmino, Paul J. (1991b). *Learning Preference Assessment facilitator guide*. King of Prussia, PA: Organization Design and Development.

Guglielmino, Paul J. & Murdick, Robert G. (1997). Self-directed learning: The quiet revolution in corporate training and development. *SAM Advanced Management Journal*, Summer, pp. 10–18.

Knowles, Malcolm (1975). *Self-directed learning: A guide for learners and teachers*. Chicago: Follett.

Knowles, Malcolm (1986). *Using contract learning*. San Francisco: Jossey-Bass.

Knowles, Malcolm (1990). *The adult learner. A neglected species*. Houston: Gulf Publishing.

Long, H.B. (1989). Truth unguessed and yet to be discovered: A professional's self-directed learning. In H.B. Long & Associates, *Self-directed learning: Emerging theory and practice* (pp. 125–135). Norman, OK: Oklahoma Research Center for Continuing, Professional, and Higher Education of the University of Oklahoma.

Long, H.B. (1990). Psychological control in self-directed learning. *International Journal of Lifelong Education*, 9(4), 331–38.

Long, H.B. (1991). Challenges in the study and practice of self-directed learning. In H. B. Long & Associates, *Self-directed learning: Consensus and conflict* (pp. 11–28). Norman, OK: Oklahoma Research Center for Continuing, Professional, and Higher Education of the University of Oklahoma.

Long, H.B. & Ageykum, S. (1988). Self-directed learning: Assessment and validation. In H.B. Long & Associates, *Self-directed learning: Application and theory* (pp. 253–266). Athens, GA: Adult Education Department, University of Georgia.

Long, H.B. & Morris, S.(1995). Self-directed learning in business and industry: A review of the literature 1983–1993. In H.B. Long & Associates (Eds.), *New dimensions in self-directed learning.* Norman, OK: College of Education, University of Oklahoma.

McCune, S.K. (1989). A meta-analytic study of adult self-direction in learning: A review of the research from 1977 to 1987 (Doctoral dissertation, Texas A&M University, 1988). *Dissertation Abstracts International*, 1989, 49, 3237.

McCune, S.K., Guglielmino, L.M., & Garcia, G. (1990). Adult self-direction in learning: A preliminary meta-analytic investigation of research using the Self-Directed Learning Readiness Scale. In H.B. Long & Associates, *Advances in self-directed learning research* (pp. 145–156). Norman, OK: Oklahoma Research Center for Continuing, Professional, and Higher Education of the University of Oklahoma.

Merriam, S.B. (1993). An update on adult learning theory. *New Directions for Adult and Continuing Education*, Spring, No. 57. San Francisco: Jossey-Bass.

Merriam, S. & Brockett, R. (1997). *The profession and practice of adult education.* San Francisco: Jossey-Bass.

Piskurich, George M. (1993). *Self-directed learning.* San Francisco: Jossey-Bass.

Senge, Peter M. (1990). *The fifth discipline: The art and practice of the learning organization.* New York: Doubleday.

Tough, A. (1979). *The adult's learning projects* (2nd ed.). Toronto: Ontario Institute for Studies in Education.

Watkins, K. & Marsick, V. (1993). *Sculpting the learning organization: Lessons in the art and science of systematic change.* San Francisco: Jossey-Bass.

CHAPTER 5

Knowledge Capture & Transfer

It is important for senior management to determine the essential knowledge underlying its business. This process can be facilitated by an OL consultant, but it requires senior management commitment.

Senior management must start by answering the following questions:

1. Who are we? What's our purpose?
2. What's our strategic plan, in a nutshell?
3. What do our customers expect from us?
4. What can we do to exceed customer expectations?
5. What do we need to know about customers to build long-term relationships?

Once essential business knowledge has been identified, a knowledge management (KM) system can be designed to capture and transfer that essential knowledge.

CODIFICATION VS. PERSONALIZATION

Hansen, Nohria, and Tierney (2001) studied management consulting firms (where knowledge is the core asset) and found two different types of KM systems, both of which were operating successfully.

At firms specializing in relatively "standardized" solutions to common problems (represented by Ernst & Young) a codification KM system is used. Codifiable knowledge is knowledge that can be easily articulated.

At firms specializing in "customized" solutions to uncommon problems (represented by McKinsey & Company), a personalization KM system is used. Personalization KM systems focus on tacit knowledge. Tacit knowledge is knowledge that cannot be easily articulated.

Hansen et al. (2001) drew two conclusions about the choice of a KM system: the choice "must be driven by the company's competitive strategy" and "trying to pursue both can quickly undermine a business" (p. 62). Based upon my own consulting experience, I believe they are right on both counts.

The Hansen et al. (2001) findings have applications far beyond management consulting firms. The implications are relevant in every industry. Every organization must determine its strategic plan, identify the critical knowledge needed to implement the plan, and then choose either a codification or a personalization KM system.

Codification Systems

To some degree, every organization needs to codify knowledge, but choosing a 50/50 codification/personalization mix is overly simplistic and inefficient (more about "straddling" later in this chapter).

Codification KM systems are appropriate for standardized processes and procedures. Once the process or procedure has been codified, it is stored in a database, which can then be accessed over and over. Obviously, computers and specialized KM software are critical here.

Hansen et al. (2001) referred to the codification KM strategy as using a "people-to-document" approach (p. 64). Their terminology corresponds to Nonaka's (1991; Nonaka & Takeuchi, 1995) concept of converting tacit knowledge (knowledge that cannot be easily articulated) to explicit knowledge.

The codification KM system separates the knowledge from the person who developed it. Once the knowledge has been extracted from the person, it can be stored in an electronic database for subsequent retrieval and reuse by other organizational members, without any need for contacting the person who developed it. This system is, therefore, highly efficient for codifiable (explicit) knowledge.

Ernst & Young (E&Y) appears to have mastered the codification KM approach. E&Y's Center for Business Knowledge is staffed by 250 people who manage an electronic database that supports 40 practice areas. E&Y's large financial investment has been justified by an organizational culture that has utilized its KM system to fulfill client needs.

The goal of any codification KM system is to connect people to reusable codified knowledge. The system must efficiently codify, store, and disseminate knowledge that is critical in serving the needs of customers (as defined in the strategic plan).

Limitations of Codification Systems

An effective codification KM system needs a gatekeeping function to determine what should be included in the database. Seely-Brown and Duguid (2001) make a distinction between "the way matters are formally organized" (policies and procedures) and "the way things actually get done" (practice). Real-life practice is what should be codified; "the way things actually get done" (p. 47).

Practice is typically spontaneous, improvised, and driven by tacit knowledge. The question a gatekeeper must ask is, *Does the documentation truly reflect real-life practice?* Frequently, experts who work together use tacit knowledge in addition to the explicit steps. This tacit knowledge, shared only between the experts, creates what Ackerman (2000) calls the "social-technical gap." Ackerman believes many of the social aspects of work cannot be captured by current technology.

I believe there is also the assumption that most tasks follow a predictable process, but in reality, it's the improvisations that make the expert a master. Seely-Brown and Duguid (2001) speak of documentation as "maps" and ask "what to do when one falls off the map?" (p. 52). This is where the expert's tacit knowledge kicks-in.

Another difficult question is, *What knowledge is significant?* "What one person thinks useful others find flaky, idiosyncratic, incoherent, redundant, or just plain stupid" (Seely-Brown & Duguid, 2001, p. 56). The gatekeeping function is critical for maintaining an effective codification KM system.

Finally, A.D. Marwick of IBM Research believes, "Information overload occurs when the quality of decisions is reduced because the decision maker spends time reviewing more information than is needed, instead of reflecting and making the decision." So, a codification KM system should be evaluated based upon how well it selects information from multiple sources to enhance human decision making.

Personalization Systems

While most organizations can benefit from the KM codification software now available, codification is effective only for explicit knowledge (knowledge that can be easily articulated). Tacit knowledge stubbornly defies capture by codification KM systems.

Tacit knowledge, which is often the most valuable knowledge in the organization, is not easily articulated or codified. "Personalization" KM systems are needed to manage this elusive creature.

Personalization KM systems are appropriate when the strategic plan focuses on providing clients with customized solutions for unique problems.

By its nature, tacit knowledge cannot be easily separated from the individual who created it. Since tacit knowledge is closely tied to its creator, a person-to-person approach (instead of the person-document-person approach of a codification system) must be utilized.

Computers in a personalization KM system are used as a locator of the person with the needed knowledge, instead of for storage of the knowledge itself. The knowledge remains "stored" with the individual who developed it.

Strategic management consulting firms (e.g., McKinsey & Company, Bain & Company, and Boston Consulting) encourage one-on-one discussions and brainstorming sessions to transfer deep insights into unique client problems. Personalization KM systems require large investments to create and support internal networks of experts. McKinsey has a directory of experts; Bain has a people-finder database. Databases in these firms provide the names of the professionals with the knowledge, not the knowledge itself.

Documents in personalization KM systems are used to simply "get up to speed" before meeting with the expert. The higher-level, tacit knowledge is transferred during the face-to-face meeting.

Personalization KM systems should focus on leading-edge tacit knowledge, beyond the codified knowledge. Reading all the codified knowledge in the field should be done before taking the time of the person who has developed the higher-level tacit knowledge.

Practice Log 5.1: The Open-Source Community
David Beitler, CCNA, believes the broader business community could benefit by understanding how the Open-Source community manages knowledge in the tech world. Open-Source practitioners write code that may be freely used and modified by other practitioners. (Part of the glue that holds the Open-Source community together is the members' shared value concerning the open access to knowledge.)

In the Open-Source community, a Linux user group frequently serves as a crossroads (and a source of guidance) for multiple user groups and websites. When an individual approaches the Linux user group with a problem, he or she is directed to a sub-community website for a specific project. At the website, the developer of the software and user community maintain documents (Readme files, HowTo files, and FAQ files) for explicit knowledge, and discussion space (forums, newsgroups, and chatrooms) for tacit knowledge exchange.

The Open-Source community offers documents to get new members up to speed. These new members are then encouraged to become active participants in the development of higher-level, tacit, community knowledge.

Straddling

Hansen et al. (2001) found, "Companies that use knowledge effectively pursue one strategy predominantly and use the second strategy to support the first. We think of this as an 80–20 split" (p. 76). While this strategy does not seem correct intuitively, my consulting experience supports their conclusion. Companies dividing resources equally between the two approaches, without being clear about what strategic knowledge they need, invariably fail at both.

The proper mix is a critical decision. The knowledge needed to fulfill the organization's strategic plan is the starting point, and guiding light, for this process. For example, a strategic plan focusing on high-end customers paying high fees for customized solutions demands a personalized KM system. These customers will not be happy with the standardized solutions stored in the codification KM system. And, of course, an equally viable strategic plan might focus on customers who are content with standardized solutions at a lower fee. That strategic plan justifies a large investment in equipment and software to support a codification system.

Hansen et al. (2001) go on to say, "Although it is important to avoid straddling, an exclusive focus on one strategy is also unwise. Companies pursuing the personalization model should have a modest electronic document system" (p. 79). I would like to offer some additional guidance here. The personalization system should be built on top of the codification system. Companies should codify as much explicit knowledge as possible first. This allows person-to-person meetings to focus on higher-level tacit knowledge. Obviously, companies will vary in the amount of knowledge that can be codified. Nevertheless, codify first.

Determining the Primary KM Strategy

Tactics should always flow from strategy. Determining a primary KM approach, codification or personalization, is a strategic decision. Senior management's clearly articulated competitive strategy should drive the determination of a primary KM strategy.

At the beginning of this chapter, I listed five questions senior management must answer. If these five questions are not already clearly addressed, the OL consultant should facilitate a discussion to answer them.

To my five questions, Hansen et al. (2001, pp. 80–81) add the following helpful questions:

1. Is the company's product standardized or customized?
2. Is the company's product mature or innovative?
3. Does the company rely on explicit or tacit knowledge to solve problems?

Of course, the decision is complicated in reality because of multiple products and multiple customer bases, but you can see the importance of their questions. Different product lines and different business units may require different primary KM strategies.

Rewards

Maximizing the effectiveness of the KM system requires rewarding high-quality contributions to the system. The two types of KM strategies require two different reward systems.

At Ernst & Young, consultants are evaluated on multiple dimensions. One dimension is their contribution to the firm's codification KM system. The consultants are encouraged to write down their knowledge for inclusion in the firm's electronic database. Of course, quality of the contributions must be assessed in addition to quantity.

At Bain & Company, consultants are evaluated on how much direct help they provide for fellow consultants. The perceived value of these contributions dramatically affects a consultant's annual pay.

Keep in mind that money is not the only reward. A reward is anything that is of value to the recipient. Recognition is a powerful reward. Attaching the individual's name to an idea is very powerful. Seely-Brown and Duguid (2001) point out that scientists regularly contribute to the scientific community and "build social capital through the quality of their input" (p. 58).

COMMUNITIES OF PRACTICE

If the organization requires a personalization KM strategy to capture and transfer knowledge to support its business strategy, communities of practice (CPs) should be part of the organization's KM system.

A community of practice (CP) is a group of peers who share a passion for a particular field of knowledge. They are informally bound and meet together face-to-face or electronically. While they may share books and other documents (codified knowledge), the primary focus of their meetings is the sharing of experiences and new ideas (tacit knowledge) that members can use in practice.

Origins of the Concept

The term "community of practice" is credited to Etienne Wenger, but he gives the credit to his colleague Jean Lave (an act of grace and humility rarely seen in the academic or business world).

Lave and Wenger (1991) did research for their first book with the initial intention of "rescuing the idea of apprenticeship" (p. 29). After studying various apprenticeship arrangements (e.g., midwives, tailors, and meat cutters), they emerged with an appreciation for the social aspects of learning. They found that much of the learning was taking place through peer discussions (peer to peer), rather than from the master's teaching (master to student).

In his academic book, entitled *Communities of Practice*, Wenger (1998, p. 3) accuses our educational system of being based on incorrect assumptions. He lists the following four false assumptions:

1. learning is an individual process,

2. learning has a beginning and an end,

3. learning is best separated from the rest of our activities,

4. learning is the result of teaching.

Clearly, corporate training and development has been based on the same assumptions. The ongoing social interaction of professional peers should be encouraged and supported by our organizations, not stifled. The learning process should be integrated into practice, not separated from it.

In my opinion, social interaction between seasoned professionals is even more important than it is between apprentices because the seasoned professionals are working with higher-level tacit knowledge.

The Value of CPs

CPs provide value in multiple forms to many groups. The beneficiaries include the individual members, the sponsoring organization, and the profession or trade.

A CP provides value to the professional development process of its individual members. Members develop a common body of knowledge, a common set of practices, and a common set of values. In addition, CPs provide:

- access to expertise
- connection to the field's growing body of knowledge
- a forum for sharing problems
- awareness of employment opportunities
- enhanced professional reputation
- personal relationships
- a sense of common identity

CPs are also very valuable to their sponsoring organizations. They can serve as the primary development method for the organization's professional staff, as they do at American Management Systems and the World Bank. CPs also provide:

- critical knowledge to support business strategy
- diagnosis and solutions for business problems
- higher quality decisions
- synergies across organizational units
- reduced time and costs
- forecasts for new developments
- analysis and feasibility of alternative strategies/tactics
- higher retention rates for professionals (more on this later)

Finally, CPs clearly promote leading-edge thinking in the profession or trade. "Communities of practice are in the best position to codify knowledge because they can combine its tacit and explicit aspects" (Wenger et al., 2002, p.9).

The cumulative nature of the knowledge in any field today is growing so rapidly it is almost impossible for any single individual to master it. The need for multiple perspectives (a collective approach) is a critical contribution of CPs to any field. (See Wenger, 1998, pp. 86–102 and 134–148 for further discussion of the collective nature of learning.)

The Structure of CPs

In their practitioner-targeted book, *Cultivating Communities of Practice*, Wenger, McDermott, and Snyder (2002) state, "Communities of practice are a practical way to frame the task of managing knowledge" (p. x). CPs provide an infrastructure for the transfer of tacit knowledge.

CPs should complement the existing organizational structure, not replace it. Project teams should be used to complete specific tasks. Formal work groups should be given the responsibility for delivery of a product or service. The sole purpose of the CP should be to capture and transfer knowledge.

CPs at their best are self-organizing; passionate volunteers make the best members. By their nature, they tend to resist supervision or interference from management.

So, can organizational leaders do anything to help create and nurture these free-flowing CPs? The answer is yes. Management cannot mandate CPs, but management can identify potential CPs and provide an infrastructure to support them (Wenger & Snyder, 2001).

Some organizations provide substantial support for their CPs. American Management Systems (AMS) and the World Bank have "adopted the community of practice as the foundation for their knowledge management strategy" (Wenger & Snyder, 2001, p. 13). These two organizations contribute large amounts of time and money to support their CPs. Both organizations believe it's a good investment.

While corporate universities (discussed in a later chapter) provide an umbrella for all organizational learning activities, CPs are the structure necessary for work *in the trenches*. "Conventional structures do not address knowledge-related problems as effectively as they do problems of performance and accountability" (Wenger et al., 2002, p. 11). Knowledge-related problems are effectively handled through the CP structure.

Wenger et al. (2002, p.27) suggest structuring or building the CP around three fundamental elements: domain, community, and practice.

The domain of the CP defines the common ground, or set of issues, that brings the members together. Initially, the domain may be the only value to the new members. (A sense of community develops subsequently.) Therefore, the domain must be clearly defined. The domain delineates the boundaries of the CP. "Knowing the boundaries and the leading edge of the domain enables members to decide exactly what is worth sharing" and "to recognize the potential in tentative or half-baked ideas" (Wenger et al., 2002, p. 28). If the CP's domain has strategic relevance, it is critical that the organization recognize its importance and provide support.

The community element is essential for trust and camaraderie to develop. Without this element, members will be unwilling to share ideas, admit ignorance, or ask for help. The importance of open, honest, and trusting relationships in professional development is discussed in detail in Whetten's (2000) work. The sense of "community identity" brings members to the table even when they don't have a burning issue to discuss. This social bond becomes as strong, or stronger, than the domain.

The element of "practice" distinguishes the CP from a mere social group. CPs provide critical practice support. "Members use each other as sounding boards, build on each other's ideas, and provide a filtering mechanism to deal with knowledge overload" (Wenger et al., 2002, p. 34). The majority of the CP members must be seasoned practitioners. CPs are not for novices. Novices should be devoting their time to the codified knowledge in the field (e.g., books and articles). Ideally, seasoned professionals should bring their real-world problems to the CP, gather ideas and advice, and then apply the ideas and advice in their practice. After application, these professionals should report their experiences back to the CP. McDermott (1999) discusses this point in more detail; he refers to it as "double-knit."

Cultivating CPs

Zemke (1999) quotes Senge as saying, "[S]ignificant innovations must be diffused through informal, self-organizing networks, through horizontal communities of practice. How you strengthen these communities is the key to how you disseminate innovation and maintain the innovators" (p. 49).

We tend to think of CPs as self-organizing, spontaneous entities that are outside the control of management. There is certainly some truth in that. But an organization's management, once convinced on the value of CPs, can do much to cultivate its CPs.

Wenger et al. (2002) offer seven design principles for all of us to be aware of. I will summarize them here. They begin by saying, "Because communities of practice are organic, designing them is more a matter of shepherding their evolution than creating them from scratch. Design elements should be catalysts for a community's natural evolution" (p. 51).

New CPs can be created from currently existing personal networks. Many potential CPs are already linked by electronic bulletin boards or memberships in professional societies.

It's also true that "Only insiders can appreciate the issues at the heart of the domain, the knowledge that is important to share, the challenges their field faces, and the latent potential in emerging ideas and techniques," but "it often takes an outsider perspective to help members see the possibilities" (Wenger et al., 2002, p. 54). This role of a consultant/coach is very valuable to the CP and to the sponsoring organization.

Interestingly, Lave and Wenger (1991) emphasize the importance of inviting different levels of participation. Unlike a work team that requires high levels of commitment to complete a task on time, CPs are not task-oriented. "Peripheral" members benefit from watching debates between core members, and may eventually become core or active members themselves. Wenger et al. suggest, "Rather than force participation, successful communities 'build benches' for those on the sidelines" (2002, p. 57).

Successful CPs must provide both public and private space. Public space includes the large events that are open to all members. Private space allows time for one-on-one relationships (e.g., during breaks, between meetings). "Every phone call, e-mail exchange, or problem-solving conversation strengthens the relationships within the community" (Wenger et al., 2002, p. 59). The community coordinator should "work this space" between meetings. (More on the role of community coordinator later.)

CPs should be maintained as a "neutral space" (Oldenberg's term), separate from job responsibilities. "Unlike team members, community members can offer advice on a project with no risk of getting entangled in it; they can listen to advice with no obligation to take it" (Wenger et al., 2002, p. 61).

The Community Coordinator

I used to believe planning and structuring were the enemies of the informal, volunteer-natures of CPs. I was the member of two energetic CPs. The free-flowing knowledge appeared to be completely spontaneous, without any planning, and without any leadership. How naive! I was blissfully unaware of the role of the community coordinator.

Studies by both the American Productivity & Quality Center (1999) and the Corporate Executive Board (1996) found the role of community coordinator to be critical for CP success. Wenger et al. (2002, p. 80) lists the key functions of the community coordinator:

- identifying important issues of the domain
- planning and facilitating community events
- linking members (by crossing unit boundaries and brokering knowledge assets)
- fostering development of individual members
- building the "practice" or knowledge base (lessons learned, best practices, tools and methods, learning events)
- assessing the health of the community

Obviously, the community coordinator must have a high level of commitment. Substantial organizational support may be necessary to fulfill this commitment. McKinsey gives its coordinators ("practice leaders") status and budgetary authority to maximize the work of its CPs (Wenger et al., 2002, p. 248).

Community coordinators do not have to be the leading experts in the field. They do need to be passionate about the knowledge domain and well-respected. An ideal candidate for this position is a midcareer professional who believes strongly in the value of networking. Interpersonal skills are a must.

Life Stages of CPs

While a detailed discussion of the stages of CP development is beyond the scope of this book, Wenger et al. (2002) devote two chapters to the subject, I would like to share a few brief comments here.

CPs are organic, life-like entities. Birth, growth, and death are natural for CPs. Wenger et al. (2002) speak of five stages of CP development (potential, coalescing, maturing, stewardship, and transformation). Every community coordinator must be able to identify the current stage of his or her CP.

Wenger et al. (2002) summarize their comments by saying, "[H]aving a sense of stages and associated issues helps you foresee problems you are likely to face, understand the changing needs of the community, and take appropriate action" (p. 70).

Summary

Unfortunately, the term "knowledge management" (KM) has been frequently associated with codification only. Codification KM systems focus on codifying explicit knowledge for storage in electronic databases. Most of my clients have a need to codify more of their standard operating procedures (SOPs). These codified SOPs can then be made available for use by all organizational members worldwide.

Codification should be the starting point for any organization's KM strategy. *Then* senior management, with the guidance of an OL consultant, must determine how the organization will develop and transfer its tacit knowledge. Tacit knowledge, by its nature, defies codification.

Personalization KM systems (including communities of practice) must be understood and utilized to maximize the value of the organization's tacit knowledge. This process requires hard work. But the reward is a sustainable competitive advantage.

REFERENCES

Ackerman, M.S. (2000). The intellectual challenge of CSCW: The gap between social requirements and technical feasibility. *Human-Computer Interaction*, 15, 179–203.

American Productivity & Quality Center (1999). *Creating a knowledge-sharing culture*. Houston: APQC.

Corporate Executive Board (1996). Building sustainable advantage: Community of practice networks. In *Heart of the enterprise: Core competencies and the renaissance of the large corporation.* Washington, DC: Corporate Executive Board, Corporate Leadership Council, pp. 171–192.

Hansen, M., Nohria, N., & Tierney, T. (2001). What's your strategy for managing knowledge? Chapter in *Harvard Business Review on Organizational Learning.* Boston, MA: Harvard Business School Publishing.

Lave, J. & Wenger, E. (1991). *Situated learning.* Cambridge, UK: Cambridge University Press.

McDermott, R. (1999). Learning across teams: How to build communities of practice in team organizations. *Knowledge Management Review,* May–June, 8, 32–38.

Nonaka, I. (1991). *The knowledge creating company.* Harvard Business Review, 69, 96–104, November–December.

Nonaka, I. & Takeuchi, H. (1995). *The knowledge creating company.* Oxford, UK: Oxford University Press.

Seely-Brown, J. & Duguid, P. (2001). Balancing act: How to capture knowledge without killing it. Chapter in *Harvard Business Review on Organizational Learning.* Boston, MA: Harvard Business School Publishing.

Wenger, E. (1998). *Communities of practice: Learning, meaning, and identity.* Cambridge, UK: Cambridge University Press.

Wenger, E., McDermott, R., & Snyder, W.M. (2002). *Cultivating communities of practice.* Boston: Harvard Business School Publishing.

Wenger, E. & Snyder, W.M. (2001). Communities of practice: The organizational frontier. Chapter in *Harvard Business Review on Organizational Learning.* Boston, MA: Harvard Business School Publishing.

Whetten, D. (2000). What matters most. *Academy of Management Journal,* 26, 2, p. 176.

Zemke, R. (1999). Why organizations still aren't learning. *Training,* September.

CHAPTER 6

Management & Professional Development

In recent years, too much emphasis has been placed on leadership development. Developing the top level, the "C-level" (CEO, COO, CFO, CIO, CMO), of the organization is still important, of course. But the grand visions of leaders (the current focus of leadership development) must be translated into bottom line results. Grand plans must be implemented by the organization's managers and professional staff.

Grand visions and plans alone will not support stock prices for long. In their recent book entitled *Execution*, Bossidy and Charan (2002) emphasize the importance of getting things done. They stress the critical factors of accountability and responsibility. Implementing (or executing) the grand plan is as important as creating it. In a time period when leadership has been romanticized, we need to reconsider what line managers and staff professionals actually need to implement the organization's strategic plan.

In this chapter, we will discuss management and professional development. In traditional organizational design theory, we speak of the "line" as the makers of the product, and the "staff" as the departments and individuals who support those who make the product.

For our purposes, we will use the term "management development" to refer to the learning and development programs designed for individuals who are responsible for the performance of the line (the making of the product). We will use the term "professional development" to refer to the learning and development programs designed for staff professionals who are responsible for supporting the line. The organization's staff includes in-house professionals such as IT professionals, accountants, financial analysts, HR professionals (including trainers), and legal staff.

Literally billions of dollars are spent annually on training and development. It is important, for our purposes, to make a clear distinction between "training" and "development."

"Training" involves the facilitation of *skills acquisition* by organizational members. Skills, including how to run the widget-making machine, how to prepare financial reports, or how to calculate the costs involved in a specific manufacturing process, require training.

"Development" is aimed at the managers and in-house professionals of the organization. Managers and professionals must possess the knowledge, skills, and attitudes (KSAs) to work with complex people and conceptual problems—under considerable pressure. The necessary managerial and professional KSAs can be acquired in a variety of ways.

It is important for organizations to think of management and professional development (M&PD) systematically. M&PD should not be simply hit-or-miss training sessions offered by outside vendors or a bookshelf full of canned courses.

An effective M&PD system contains the following three elements:

1. assessment
2. development
3. performance management

Let's look at each element in detail.

Assessment

Assessment is concerned with the needs of the organization, the needs of the individual, and the "fit" between the two sets of needs. Assessment helps maximize both organizational effectiveness and individual effectiveness.

First and foremost, the manager or in-house professional must understand the organization in which he or she works. Managers and professionals must have a clear understanding of the organization's vision and strategy, its structure, its culture, and its processes. This clarity allows the individual to focus his or her efforts on strategically important tasks.

The assessment process should be designed to help the individual develop an awareness of his or her personal preferences and of how he or she interacts with others. This awareness is critical for developing the individual's strengths and ameliorating his or her weaknesses.

In-House vs. External Assessment

Assessment can be done in-house or by independent assessment firms. Typically, only large organizations have the budget and expertise to perform this function in-house. Many companies prefer to outsource this function to professional consultants or firms that conduct management assessments for a living. One example is the Center for Creative Leadership (CCL) here in Greensboro, North Carolina.

Assessment Instruments

Assessment involves the use of multiple assessment instruments that provide feedback for the purpose of increasing an individual's self-awareness.

Most of these instruments require rigorous training and certification of the consultant before purchasing and using them. Certification of the consultant helps to assure both the organization and the individual manager or professional of appropriate instrument use and interpretation.

I recommend *not* using the free internet instruments that require the manager or professional to interpret the feedback data without guidance. Paying consultants who are certified to use and interpret instruments (instruments that have been subjected to rigorous validity studies) is a wise investment of the organization's money. Misinterpretation or invalid instruments do more harm than good.

Let me introduce you to a few of the instruments I currently use in practice. Please note that there are many more available to practitioners, but these five will be valuable tools in your toolbox:

1. MBTI
2. FIRO Element B
3. KAI
4. SDLRS
5. CCAI

One of the best known of the assessment (or preference) instruments is the Myers-Briggs Type Indicator (MBTI). The MBTI provides the manager with awareness about his or her preferences in four areas:

1. external vs. internal focus (extraversion/introversion)
2. perceiving, or data gathering method (sensing/intuiting)
3. judging, or decision making criteria (thinking/feeling)
4. scheduled vs. spontaneous approach (judging/perceiving)

According to the original theory, developed by German-Swiss psychologist Carl Jung, extraverts (E) prefer the external world. Extraverts process information by talking about it. They are energized by people. Introverts (I) process information internally, by quietly thinking about it. Introverts have to get away from people to "recharge their batteries" (don't take this behavior personally if you are an extravert).

Sensors (S) depend on their five senses. What they can see, hear, smell, touch, or taste is "real." They are focused on the here-and-now. Intuitors (N) are more concerned with ideas, concepts, and possibilities. They tend to focus on the future.

Thinkers (T) and feelers (F) make decisions differently. Thinkers work hard to develop logical, linear, rational arguments to support universal principles that should apply to everyone. Feelers believe that process is too cold. They want to talk about how individuals will be affected by the decisions. Thinkers don't like exceptions to the rules; feelers don't mind exceptions. Feelers believe decisions should be made on a case-by-case basis.

The judging (J) and perceiving (P) dichotomy is concerned with the use of time. Js want events to be highly structured; an agenda or to-do list is important to them. Ps believe the spontaneous use of time is best; agendas and to-do lists are restricting to them.

I usually use the MBTI first with clients, before moving on to other instruments. Most client members I've worked with find the MBTI interesting and fun. And because the MBTI has been subjected to rigorous reliability and validity testing, most managers don't argue with the feedback. The latest version, MBTI Form M, is especially well received by clients.

The FIRO Element B is part of a series of instruments developed by Dr. Will Schutz. The Element B is especially appropriate in management and professional assessment. The Element B offers feedback concerning how the individual prefers to interact with others. Like other preference instruments, this one does not measure skills; it simply reveals preferences.

The FIRO Element B focuses on an individual's preferences for inclusion, control, and openness in human interactions. The instrument provides feedback on four aspects of each of these three preferences: two concerning "give" (now vs. wanted) and two concerning "receive" (now vs. wanted). Large differences between giving/receiving-now and giving/receiving-wanted indicate that the individual is experiencing stress concerning that particular aspect of human interaction.

The FIRO Element B is also a great team-building tool. Since everybody has different needs/wants for inclusion, control, and openness, it is helpful to understand the needs/wants of other team members. I have used this instrument in practice with intact teams and new teams. With dysfunctional teams this instrument usually reveals large difference in either inclusion, control, or openness needs.

Another valuable tool in management assessment is the Kirton Adaptor/Innovator Instrument (KAI). Unfortunately, the KAI is still not widely used in the U.S. The KAI is the brainchild of Dr. Michael Kirton, a British researcher and practitioner.

Kirton believes all human beings are creative, but he believes they express their creativity differently based on how they prefer to change (improve) things. Adaptors (A) want to change things slowly, incrementally, one-step at a time. Adaptors like the tweaking involved in a continuous improvement process, such as TQM. Innovators (I) like quick, quantum, dramatic change. Innovators like the idea of re-engineering or radically changing the whole system.

There are also "bridges," like me. Bridges score in the middle of Kirton's scale; they can appreciate both approaches. I have two close friends who are both very intelligent. She is an adaptor; she wants slow, incremental, cautious change. He speaks in terms of "blowing up the system" and starting from scratch. I enjoy both of them, but they can't stand to be around each other.

The KAI is very helpful because it reveals potential problems between extreme adaptors and extreme innovators. Awareness of these differences allows for alternative responses.

The Self-Directed Learning Readiness Scale (SDLRS) is a valuable instrument in both management development and professional development (Beitler, 2000). We discussed the SDLRS at length in Chapter Four. For M&PD purposes, the SDLRS helps in designing a customized learning and development plan for the individual.

The Cross-Cultural Adaptability Index (CCAI) is becoming increasingly important in M&PD as domestic companies become international organizations. I have done a lot of work with my colleagues in preparing and supporting expatriate managers and professionals for foreign assignments. Managers or professionals with low adaptability scores do poorly on foreign assignments, regardless of how talented or well-trained they are (Chuprina & Durr, 2001). We will discuss this important issue further in Chapter Seven.

DEVELOPMENT

Developmental activities for managers and professionals fall into several categories:

Coaching/Mentoring

Behavior Modeling

Experiential/Sensitivity Training

Job Rotation

Cross-Cultural Training

Career Planning

Coaching/Mentoring

Coaching provides guidance for specific skill development. The role of coach can be performed by an in-house or independent coach.

Mentoring is broader in scope than coaching. Mentoring usually involves an older (more experienced) manager taking a younger manager under his or her wing. Mentoring goes beyond specific skill development to include guidance for career and personal development. Successful mentoring involves a mentor who is personally committed to the success of a protégé. Effective mentoring relationships can be encouraged or supported by the company but not forced.

Behavior Modeling

Behavior modeling can be done with individuals or with groups. It is based on Bandura's (1977) Social Learning Theory, which assumes the following about individuals:

1. they must perceive the connection between their behavior and certain outcomes,

2. they must desire the outcomes, and

3. they must believe they can accomplish them.

Behavior modeling involves:

1. discovering specific behaviors that lead to success,
2. watching a model demonstrate the behavior (the model must be somebody the manager can relate to), and
3. practicing the behavior under the guidance of the expert.

In behavior modeling sessions, videotaping can be used to capture role-playing exercises. The videotapes can then be reviewed and critiqued.

Experiential/Sensitivity Training

While the use of experiential and sensitivity training has declined in recent years, it may still have a place in some organizations. Many experiential or sensitivity exercises fail to transfer learning back to the job.

A popular form of sensitivity training during the 1970s was the T-group. T-groups were unstructured, agenda-less group sessions where feelings and reactions of group members were openly discussed. The goals of the sessions included increased self-awareness, sensitivity to others, and improved communication.

Since T-groups frequently involve intense emotional reactions, I recommend against their use unless a trained psychologist facilitates the session. Generally speaking, T-groups are inappropriate for business or professional groups. M&PD should not be confused with psychotherapy.

Other experiential exercises (such as wilderness journeys and white-water rafting) should be seen as fun, not necessarily developmental. They can lead to better relationships but rarely improve job performance.

Job Rotation

One highly effective activity for management development is job rotation. Job rotation can also be used for professional development, but the possible applications are more limited. In job rotation (unlike T-groups) it is easy to see the transferability of the experience or new learning to actual job performance improvements. Job rotation provides the manager with not only new skills (e.g., running the widget-making machine), but new insights into the world of others (e.g., understanding the viewpoint of widget-machine operators).

Cross-Cultural Training

Effective cross-cultural training is still lacking in American companies. Americans, true to their culturally insensitive stereotype, conduct cross-cultural training in an ethnocentric manner. Many of these American programs focus only on American issues (black/white, male/female). This narrow approach excludes much of the rest of the world.

I will have more to say about training managers for foreign (truly cross-cultural) assignments in the next chapter. The failure rate of American expatriate managers is extremely and unacceptably high. An effective program for expatriate manager preparation and support is critical to a global organization's success.

Career Planning

Career planning activities should be supported (financially and otherwise) by organizations because both the individual and the organization itself benefit. Managers and professionals who don't fit the organization or their jobs become increasingly dissatisfied and unproductive.

Numerous career planning activities (Schein, 1987; Lippitt, 1970; Fordyce & Weil, 1971) available for M&PD help the manager or professional understand his or her core values. Core values are what are truly important to the individual. Core values are powerful motivators.

PERFORMANCE MANAGEMENT

Effective performance management systems for managers and professionals should include two related, well-planned subsystems:

1. goal setting and performance appraisal
2. rewards and guidance counseling

Let's look first at goal setting and performance appraisals. Then, we will look at rewards to reinforce positive behavior and goal accomplishment. Finally, we will discuss the importance of providing guidance counseling for negative behavior and for failure to accomplish goals.

Goal Setting and Performance Appraisal

Performance appraisals should be based on collaboratively determined goals. Agreement on expectations must be reached during the goal setting phase. This collaborative process ensures the individual's buy-in. Actual performance should then be measured against these agreed-upon goals and expectations.

Performance appraisal should include both periodic (formal) and ongoing (informal) feedback. Work-related successes, failures, strengths, and weaknesses should be discussed openly and frankly between manager and supervisor.

The use of performance appraisals is frequently driven by legal concerns but should be considered for its important contribution to management and professional development. Some experts (including Muchinsky, 2002) believe the performance appraisal process should involve two separate meetings: one for developmental purposes and one for administrative purposes (pay raises and related issues). I agree with Muchinsky's argument for two separate meetings. The developmental benefits of performance appraisals should not be overshadowed by administrative matters.

Performance evaluation provides two types of feedback: negative and positive. Negative feedback occurs when performance does not meet expectations and goals. Negative feedback should lead to discussion about future development. Positive feedback occurs when performance meets or exceeds expectations and goals. Performance at these high levels should be reinforced with rewards.

Rewards and Guidance Counseling

"Reward systems are concerned with eliciting and reinforcing desired behaviors and work outcomes" (Cummings & Worley, 2001). Desired behaviors should be rewarded; undesired behaviors require guidance counseling. Let's discuss rewards for desired behaviors first.

The subject of rewarding and reinforcing behavior is closely related to the popular subject of motivation. Highly trained managers and professionals may still fail to meet their potential if they are not motivated.

Two types of rewards should be considered to enhance individual performance: intrinsic rewards and extrinsic rewards. A combination of both can be found in an effective reward system.

The following examples of intrinsic rewards can be made available to most individuals:

1. more decision-making authority
2. interesting assignments
3. enriched jobs

Managers and professionals are also motivated by the following extrinsic rewards:

1. pay increases and/or bonuses
2. stock options
3. gain sharing
4. promotions

Obviously, relying solely on extrinsic rewards is too expensive for companies in competitive industries. Intrinsic rewards preserve cash, plus they lead to long-term improvements in manager performance. Extrinsic rewards tend to produce only short-term performance improvements.

The key to finding motivating rewards is to identify the rewards that are most highly valued by the individual. For example, a flexible work schedule may be more motivating than a pay raise. Or an interesting job assignment (a lateral move) may be more motivating than a promotion. Identifying highly motivating rewards involves ongoing communication with the individual manager or professional. Each individual is motivated by different rewards.

Most companies still have reward systems designed by compensation experts or senior management. But "there is growing evidence that employee participation in the design and administration of a reward system can increase employee understanding and can contribute to feelings of control over and commitment to the plan" (Cummings & Worley, 2001).

While it is beyond the scope of this book, we should familiarize ourselves with the wide variety of compensation options that are available, including:

1. skill-based pay
2. performance-based pay
3. gain sharing
4. "cafeteria-style" pay packages

Finally, senior managers must be willing and able to give constructive negative feedback to managers and professionals for whom they are responsible. All of us fail at times; all of us make mistakes. We can grow and learn from these failures and mistakes if we receive proper guidance. Serving subordinates in the role of a guidance counselor is an important role. The organization should be confident that its leaders are prepared to perform this role.

SUCCESSION PLANNING

Succession planning has become a major concern for many of my clients who employ aging baby boomers considering retirement. Many of these boomers built their professional careers in a very competitive environment; they *believe* what they know is a competitive asset that must be carefully guarded.

An effective succession plan (SP) is based upon senior management's work on the following:

1. aligning the SP with the strategic plan
2. identifying key positions
3. identifying candidates for key positions
4. utilizing real-time learning for candidate development
5. assuring line ownership of the SP
6. integrating the SP with other developmental programs

Aligning with the Strategic Plan

Throughout my books and articles I stress the importance of aligning everything with the strategic plan. Succession planning is no exception.

The succession planning process should not begin with discussions about people for specific positions. The SP process must begin with discussions about the organization's strategic plan and the future needs of the organization. The organization's strategic plan is the guidepost for the entire SP process.

Organizations, and their strategic plans, are not static. They are dynamic; they are continuing to evolve. The succession plan must be aligned with the organization's evolving needs.

Changes in the strategic plan should automatically mandate a review of the succession plan. Several authors (Buckner & Slavenski, 1994; Clark & Lyness, 1991; Hall & Seibert, 1991; Rothwell, 2000) discuss the need for a succession plan that responds to changes in the strategic plan.

The critical nature of this link between the succession plan and the strategic plan calls for a thorough review of the current strategic plan. Leibman and Bruer (1994) believe the same executives who are involved in the strategic planning process should also be involved in the periodic succession planning and management development reviews.

Allison (1993) lamented that succession planning in most organizations was not linked with long-term planning or strategic planning. In many organizations this is still true.

A succession plan should have its own mission statement or statement of purpose that clearly articulates how the succession plan is linked to the strategic plan. Rothwell (2000, p. 103) offers a list of issues to be addressed in this statement of purpose.

The succession plan must be tailored to the needs of the specific organization. The organization's size, structure, growth rate, culture, and values must be considered. Gratton and Syrett (1990) describe four different but successful succession planning approaches.

Identifying Key Positions

Once the strategic plan has been reviewed, the next step is to identify the key positions needed to implement the plan. Positions in the organization are "key" if the loss of the people in the positions would lead to great loss or disruption.

Once the key positions are identified, the required competencies must be clearly defined. Two lists are required here: one for current and one for projected competencies. The position's required competencies will be dynamic, as are the company's product/services and customer preferences. Buckner and Slavenski (1994) recommend a shift in focus from specific to more general competencies in dynamic organizations.

Rothwell (2000) recommends merging generic management and leadership competencies with organization-specific competencies to create what he calls an "executive success profile." Organization-specific competencies must consider organizational culture, values, market position, and customer base.

Identifying Candidates

Senior managers tend to support and recommend successors similar to themselves. This strategy is not necessarily bad, unless similarity is the only criterion. Subjective and anecdotal assessments must be balanced by objective, job-relevant assessments.

Performance appraisals must be part of the process of identifying candidates. Many well-liked candidates simply do not get the job done. Bossidy and Charan (2002) discuss this situation in their popular book entitled *Execution*. An objective evaluation of results is critical. Performance appraisals must be of the 360-degree nature; supervisor-only appraisals will not suffice.

Psychological assessments (discussed earlier) and independent assessment centers are valuable contributors to candidate profiles. These assessments, along with performance appraisals, provide the raw material needed to construct the individual's developmental plan.

In the identifying candidates step, it is important to hear from the candidates themselves. What are the aspirations of the candidate? Interests? Willingness to relocate? Sometimes senior managers are surprised to learn that a candidate does not share the same aspirations and dreams as senior management. Buckner and Slavenski (1994) offer a simple solution. They believe a career-interest form can gather the needed information on career goals and life/work preferences. Clearly, this is important information to add to the other data.

Real-Time Learning

The development of candidates must emphasize "real-time" learning. While I am a big believer in the generic knowledge and skills provided by MBA programs, the company-specific and position-specific competencies must come through real-time learning.

Real-time learning includes job assignments, mentoring, and participation in communities of practice. Real-time learning activities can be planned and monitored by organizational leaders.

Real-time learning activities should be part of each candidate's learning agreement. (We discussed the collaborative creation of learning agreements in Chapter 4.) The learning agreement should align the needs and aspirations of the candidate with the needs and goals of the organization.

There is convincing evidence that managers learn best through challenging assignments (e.g., job rotation, task force membership, turnarounds). See Baldwin and Padgett (1993), Buckner and Slavenski (1994), Hinrichs and Hollenbeck (1990), and McCauley et al. (1995) for examples of how to use job assignments for professional development. Lateral moves are particularly valuable in today's flatter organizations.

Clark and Lyness (1991) report that Citicorp uses stretch assignments. Citicorp places high-potential candidates in positions in which they are no more than 60 to 70 percent qualified.

As we will discuss in the next chapter on "Expatriate Training," international companies must include foreign assignments in the candidate's real-time learning.

Line Ownership

While I agree with Rothwell (2000) who warns, "if top managers are unwilling to support a systematic approach to succession planning, it cannot succeed" (p. 49), the organization must be clear about "ownership" of the process.

Obviously, once the succession plan is established it must be delegated to someone. A common mistake is to turn over the succession plan ownership to the HR department. It must be clear to everyone that HR is a staff department serving in an internal consultant role. While staff departments can facilitate processes, line managers must take responsibility for results.

Line managers must be held responsible for identifying and developing candidates for succession. The HR professionals can serve in a valuable support role, but there should be no confusion about the line management ownership. Kramer's (1990) work is a good source for suggestions on how to encourage line ownership.

Integrating with Other Activities

Just as everything in the organization must be driven by the strategic plan, everything in the organization must be integrated with everything else.

The organization's succession plan should be integrated with selection, compensation, career planning, management development, performance appraisal, assessment, and coaching.

Rothwell (2000) suggests quarterly, individual-development plan reviews. I would suggest adding a cross-functional aspect to this quarterly review process by having senior management meetings to discuss candidates from various areas in the organization. It is very helpful for senior managers to be aware of talent throughout the organization.

Summary

The organization's M&PD and succession-planning systems should help align the efforts of the individual with the organization's goals and strategic plan. It is critical that managers and professionals understand and support the organization's strategy, structure, culture, and processes.

REFERENCES

Allison, W. (1993). The next generation of leaders. *Human Resource Professional*, Fall, pp. 30–32.

Baldwin, T. & Padgett, M. (1993). Management development: A review and commentary. In C.L. Cooper and I.T. Robertson (Eds.), *International review of industrial and organizational psychology* (Vol.8). Chichester, England: John Wiley & Sons.

Bandura, A. (1977). *Social learning theory.* Englewood Cliffs, NJ: Prentice-Hall.

Beitler, M.A. (2000). Contract learning in organizational learning and management development. In H.B. Long & Associates (Eds.), *Practice and theory in self-directed learning.* Schaumburg, IL: Motorola University Press.

Bossidy, L. & Charan, R. (2002). *Execution: The discipline of getting things done.* New York: Crown Business.

Buckner, M. & Slavenski, L. (1994). Succession planning. In W.R. Tracey (Ed.), *Human resources management and development handbook* (2nd ed.). New York: AMACOM.

Chuprina, L. & Durr, R. (2001). Implications of foreign culture and SDL on expatriate managers at Motorola, Inc. In H.B. Long & Associates (Eds.), *Self-directed learning in the new millennium*. Schaumberg, IL: Motorola University Press.

Clark, L. & Lyness, K. (1991). Succession planning as a strategic activity at Citicorp. In L.W. Foster (Ed.), *Advances in applied business strategy* (Vol.2). Greenwich, CT: JAI Press.

Cummings T.G. & Worley, C.G. (2001). *Organization development and change* (7th ed.). Cincinnati, OH: South-Western.

Fordyce, J.K. & Weil, R. (1971). *Managing with people*. Reading, MA: Addison-Wesley. (pp. 109–113)

Gratton, L. & Syrett, M. (1990). Heirs apparent: Succession strategies for the future. *Personnel Management*, 22, 1, pp. 34–38.

Hall, D. & Seibert, K. (1991). Strategic management development: Linking organizational strategy, succession planning, and managerial learning. In D.H. Montross and C.J. Shinkman (Eds.), *Career development: Theory and practice*. Springfield, IL: Charles C. Thomas.

Hinrichs, J. & Hollenbeck, G. (1990). Leadership development. In K.W. Wexley (Ed.), *Developing human resources* (Vol.5). Washington, DC: Bureau of National Affairs.

Kramer, D. (1990). Executive succession and development systems: A practical approach. In M. London, E.S. Bassman, & J.P. Fernandez (Eds.), *Human resource forecasting and strategy development: Guidelines for analyzing and fulfilling organizational needs*. Westport, CT: Quorum Books.

Leibman, M. & Bruer, R. (1994). Where there's a will there's a way. *Journal of Business Strategy*, 15, 2, March/April.

Lippitt, G. (1970). Developing life plans. *Training and Development Journal*, May, pp. 2–7.

McCauley, C., Eastman, L., & Ohlott, P. (1995). Linking management selection and development through stretch assignments. *Human Resource Management*, 34, 1, Winter.

Muchinsky, P.M. (2002). *Psychology applied to work* (7th ed.). Belmont, CA: Wadsworth/Thomson Learning.

Rothwell, W. (2000). *Effective succession planning: Ensuring leadership continuity and building talent from within* (2nd ed.). New York: AMACOM.

Schein, E.H. (1987). Individuals and careers. In J.W. Lorsch (Ed.), *Handbook of organizational behavior*. Englewood Cliffs, NJ: Prentice-Hall.

CHAPTER 7

Expatriate Training & Support

By necessity, much of the responsibility for success in international markets falls upon expatriate managers. Expatriate managers are managers working in countries other than their home countries. Successful implementation of a global business strategy requires expatriate managers with cross-cultural management skills.

HIGH FAILURE RATES

Expatriate managers, especially U.S. managers working in foreign countries, experience very high failure rates. Black and Gregersen (1999) report the following alarming findings:

1. Nearly one-third of U.S. managers sent abroad do not perform up to the expectations of their superiors.

2. Up to 20 percent of all U.S. managers sent abroad return early because of job dissatisfaction or difficulties in adjusting to a foreign country.

3. One-fourth of U.S. managers completing a foreign assignment left their company within one year after repatriation (often joining a competitor).

Perhaps even more disturbing than Black and Gregersen's findings is the fact that we have known about these appalling failure rates for many years. In January of 1990, a *Training & Development Journal* article stated, "Up to 40 percent of U.S. expatriate managers fail in their overseas assignments" (Hogan and Goodson, 1990).

In that same article, Hogan and Goodson described how Japanese companies had achieved a dramatically better success rate with their expatriate managers. They discussed one survey that stated "86 percent of multinational corporations in Japan had failure rates below 10 percent for their expatriates."

Hogan and Goodson (1990) described the typical Japanese firm's expatriate support program as follows:

1. One year before managers depart, they devote company time to studying the culture and language of the destination country.
2. In the foreign country, the expatriate managers work with mentors who are responsible directly to the head office for assisting the managers with cultural problems that arise.
3. The first-year performance appraisal form clearly indicates that the expatriate's primary job during year one is to learn about and adjust to the host country.

Hogan and Goodson (1990) recommended the following:

1. Training should aim at developing communication, leadership, conflict management, and other skills that fit the particular culture.
2. Predeparture training should be tailored to the individual manager's needs. A minimum requirement is a conversational knowledge of the host country's language.
3. The expatriate's family should receive predeparture training.
4. Sponsorship (a mentor) should provide ongoing support.

In a study involving survey responses of 72 human resource managers at multinational corporations (MNCs), 35 percent of the HR managers said cultural adaptability was the most important success factor in a foreign assignment (Dallas, 1995).

The Costs of the Problem

The costs of these expatriate management failures are very high for the managers and their companies. Managers report personal relationship problems with family members who move to the foreign country with them, and a sense of disconnect with their families and friends in their home countries. Managers also report a fear of career derailment resulting from foreign assignment failure.

The companies experience very high costs, in terms of opportunity costs and hard costs. Opportunity costs include the loss of future business and reputation in the community. The failure of a U.S. manager reinforces the stereotype of the culturally inept American.

Hard costs of these failures for U.S. companies are staggering. One American expatriate manager I interviewed reported receiving a $10,000 *per month* housing allowance from her multinational corporation (MNC) while on a two-year assignment in Tokyo. She personally added another $1,000 per month to the allowance to rent an apartment. Add the cost of several trips home per year and multiply that by several hundred expatriate managers, and you get an idea of the hard costs involved.

A Four-Phase Training Model

Researchers (Harrison, 1994; Harris and Moran, 1991) have proposed a four-phase training model for expatriate managers:

1. Self-awareness
2. General awareness of cultural differences
3. Specific knowledge acquisition
4. Specific skills training

Self-Awareness

The self-awareness phase should be designed to provide the trainees with insight into their receptiveness and propensity for successful cross-cultural assignments. There are several psychological instruments available for managers and their family members, including the Cross-Cultural Adaptability Inventory (Kelley & Meyers, 1992) and the Intercultural Sensitivity Inventory (Bhawuk & Brislin, 1992). After completing several psychological instruments, it may become clear to the manager (or to his/her supervisor) that overseas assignment may not be appropriate.

Jordan and Cartwright (1998) believe successful expatriate managers have the following attributes:

1. Emotional stability
2. Self-confidence
3. Intellectual capacity
4. Openness to new experiences
5. Relational ability
6. Linguistic skill
7. Cultural sensitivity
8. Ability to handle stress

General Awareness of Cultural Differences

The general awareness of cultural differences phase of training is now supported by an impressive body of literature. Kluckhohn and Strodtbeck (1961), Hofstede (1980, 1993), and Trompenaars (1998) provide insight into how cultures differ on various dimensions.

Kluckhohn and Strodtbeck (1961) describe six different cultural dimensions:

1. How people view humanity (good, evil, mixed)
2. How people see nature (domination, harmony, subjugation)
3. How people approach interpersonal relationships (individualistic, group, hierarchical)
4. How people view activity and achievement (being, controlling, doing)
5. How people view time (past, present, future)
6. How people view space (private, public, mixed)

Bennett (1986) believes by educating individuals to recognize their own values, they can better identify contrasts with other cultures and then apply these insights to improving cross-cultural interactions. Harrison (1994) adds, "To appreciate the differences in other cultures, trainees must understand their own culture."

Specific Knowledge Acquisition

The specific knowledge acquisition phase includes area studies, language studies, and host attitude awareness. Area studies, covering history, political system, economy, demographics, and climate are assumed to increase empathy, which will modify behavior in cross-cultural interactions (Tung, 1981).

Researchers (Copeland & Griggs, 1985; Harris & Moran, 1991) have found knowledge of the host country's language to be essential. Interestingly, an individual's level of confidence and willingness to use the host language is a greater influence on success than his or her actual level of fluency (Mendenhall & Oddou, 1985). Therefore, building the trainee's confidence and willingness is critical.

In this phase, it is important for the trainee to become aware of the attitudes he or she will face in the host country. Work-related attitudes such as productivity, dependability, pace, frequency of breaks, meeting interruptions, and deadlines vary greatly from culture to culture. Trainees must also be alerted to possible negative attitudes toward nationality, race, or gender.

Specific Skills Training

The specific skills training phase emphasizes the application and practice of the skills necessary to succeed in the foreign culture. In this phase, "trainees analyze the problem situation, diagnose the underlying cultural issues, and respond accordingly" (Harrison, 1994). Case studies, simulations, and behavior modeling allow for the application and practice of previously acquired knowledge.

One effective skills-training method is the simulated cocktail party (Earley, 1987). The interactions in this simulation require the use of greetings and introductions, etiquette, and appropriate topics for conversation. Mendenhall and Oddou (1998) believe this type of simulation forces the trainees to deal with emotions resulting from cross-cultural misunderstandings.

Harrison (1992) describes the use of behavior modeling as an effective cross-cultural training tool. Managers watch live or videotaped models demonstrating effective behaviors; then the managers rehearse the demonstrated behaviors. Trainers should be available to provide feedback.

THE BEITLER AND FRADY MODEL

Beitler and Frady's (2002) model of Expatriate Manager Assessment and Development builds upon aspects of Harrison's (1994) and Jordan and Cartwright's (1998) work. Beitler and Frady's (2002) model includes the following steps:

1. Assessment
2. Individualized Learning Agreements
3. Pre-Departure Training/Orientation
4. E-Support During the Foreign Assignment
5. Periodic Re-Assessment
6. Learning Agreement Revisions
7. On-Going E-Support

Let's briefly look at each of the seven steps in Beitler and Frady's (2002) model:

Assessment

Any management development program should begin with assessment. The assessment phase should be especially comprehensive for expatriates because of the unique KSAs required for foreign assignment. The typical management assessment instruments are helpful, but they should be supplemented with instruments such as the Cross-Cultural Adaptability Instrument (CCAI) and the Self-Directed Learning Readiness Scale (SDLRS).

Individualized Learning Agreements

The learning agreement, as detailed in Beitler (2000, 1999), should include the following:

    a. What will be learned.

    b. How will it be learned.

c. How will the learning be documented.

   d. How will the learning be evaluated.

Pre-Departure Training/Orientation

At a minimum, this process should include general awareness of the culture and basic language skills. It is important to include spouses and dependents, as well as the expatriate managers, in this phase.

E-Support During Foreign Assignment

This step is critical in the Beitler and Frady (2002) model. Training and development for the expatriate manager only *begins* in the pre-departure phase. Ongoing support is necessary for success. The expatriate manager will need to acquire additional KSAs after arriving in the host country.

In the pre-departure phase, managers can acquire knowledge (K) through classroom learning, skills (S) through daily mentoring, and proper attitudes (A) through face-to-face counseling sessions.

During foreign assignment, classroom learning must become E-learning, daily mentoring must become E-mentoring, and face-to-face counseling must become E-counseling. The technology is now available to support E-learning, E-mentoring, and E-counseling (see Beitler & Frady, 2002). Today's global organizations must utilize that technology.

Periodic Re-Assessment

This activity is very important for the success of a foreign assignment. The expatriate manager should receive as much feedback as possible. Guidance from a host country supervisor or sponsor would be ideal but is not always possible. At a minimum, peers and subordinates should be surveyed for input.

Learning Agreement Revisions

New learning agreements should immediately follow the periodic performance reviews. Plans for enhancing strengths and ameliorating weaknesses should be clearly written.

Ongoing E-Support

Ongoing support in the forms of E-learning, E-mentoring, and E-counseling is an investment that will yield substantial returns for the organization. This support should be well planned and monitored for continuous improvement.

Who's Involved?

A comprehensive expatriate support system should include all four of the following:

1. Manager
2. Spouse
3. Dependents
4. Host-country sponsor

E-learning, E-mentoring, and E-counseling can be provided for all four stakeholders.

The Role of Technology

Knowledge created through expatriate training and support should be captured in a codified knowledge management (KM) system (see Chapter 5). This technology provides for the capturing and dissemination of individual expatriate knowledge for the benefit of the organization. Ongoing, new learning should be constantly fed into the KM system. Each part of the expatriate training and support system should be linked to the KM system.

CROSS-CULTURAL DESIGN ISSUES

Globalization does not mean the "GM-ization," or "GE-ization," or "American-ization" of business practice. Successful globalization of OL practice will involve the blending of adult learning theory with various international cultures. This outcome means that managers and OL designers must understand cultural differences and be willing to compromise on a variety of practices.

I have personally made the mistake of using the same instructional method for the same workshop in two different countries. In one country the trainees were enthusiastically engaged; in the other country I was looking at a sea of confused faces.

Fortunately for American trainers, language is becoming less of a barrier to effective training. English has become the international business language.

While language is less of a barrier, cultural expectations can still turn a learning opportunity into a bewildering and frustrating experience. In every country, individuals have acquired expectations about training design. Knowing those expectations is critical.

Capabilities & Readiness

Beyond expectations is the issue of trainee capabilities and readiness. The first summer I taught at a German university, I was told "German business schools do not use case studies." The unspoken implication was "do not use case studies in Germany."

But based upon my research into these German students, I decided to use case studies anyway. My research indicated that these students were very bright, rigorously trained, and possessed a knowledge base that was both broad and deep.

Stunned silence was the initial reaction to my suggestion that the students (in groups) would be presenting their case diagnosis and recommendations to the entire class. But after some guidance and confidence building, I was amazed by the quality of their analysis. The students seemed equally amazed at the quality of their performance.

What did I learn? I should never determine training design solely on the trainees' past experience with training methods. Learning involves getting outside of our comfort zones. There is nothing more satisfying than surprising ourselves with what we are capable of doing.

Oechsler's Research

Walter Oechsler of the University of Mannheim (Germany) has provided insight into the duality of the globalization of business and the localization (nationalization) of employment relations (Oechsler, 1999). Oechsler states, "Globalization was enhanced by the liberalization of world markets and the almost free movement of capital throughout the world. At the same time, national governments . . . still regulate their national and local employment relations" (1999, p. 97).

Oechsler (1999, p. 97) asks this question, "How does global management cope with local employment relations?" His question is important for trainers and OL consultants. How we design and conduct training must be considered in light of the prevailing political and cultural forces in each country.

While European countries will continue reconciling their economic and cultural differences, dramatic differences in employee relations (including those affecting training and development) will still exist from one EU country to another. Training efforts involving more than one country (European or otherwise) must be adjusted for these differences.

HOFSTEDE'S RESEARCH

In his 1993 seminal work on cultural values, Geert Hofstede proposed four dimensions along which societies can be classified:

1. Power Distance — the degree to which unequal distribution of power is accepted between workers and managers

2. Individualism — the degree to which individual decision making is valued

3. Uncertainty Avoidance — the degree to which uncertainty is avoided or tolerated (e.g., job security)

4. Masculinity — the degree to which society values the traditionally masculine traits of assertiveness, task achievement, and material possessions.

Figure 7.1 shows a summary of Hofstede's extremes on the four dimensions:

POWER DISTANCE

High	Low
Focus on order	Focus on equity
Well-defined hierarchies	Flat organizations
Autocratic managers	Democratic managers
Centralized power	Decentralized power

INDIVIDUALISM

High	Low
Emphasis on individual	Emphasis on group
Creative person valued	Creative person disruptive
Initiative valued	Conformity valued

UNCERTAINTY AVOIDANCE

High	Low
Focus on security	Openness to the unknown
Risk is uncomfortable	Risk equals opportunity
Defined roles	Flexible roles
Focus on rules	Quick decisions

MASCULINITY

High	Low
Men dominate	Flexible gender roles
Aggressive environment	Nurturing environment
Monetary rewards	Nonmonetary recognition

Source: Hofstede, G. (1993). Cultural constraints in management theories. *Academy of Management Executive,* 7, 81–94.

FIGURE 7.1: Hofstede's Cultural Dimensions

To date, more than 50 countries have been classified as being high, medium, or low on Hofstede's cultural dimensions. The implications of Hofstede's findings should not be underestimated. Managers and OL consultants hoping to implement changes in cultures other than their own must be able to make adjustments to accommodate for different cultural expectations.

TROMPENAARS' WORK

The work of Fons Trompenaars builds upon Hofstede's groundbreaking research. The Trompenaars' database is astonishing. The data set comprises some 50,000 cases from over 100 countries. By restricting the analysis to managers from multinational and international corporations faced with internationalizing their operations, some 30,000 comparative valid cases can be selected drawn from 55 countries. (Trompenaars and Hampden-Turner, 1998, p. 252)

Trompenaars (1998) believes, "every culture distinguishes itself from others by the specific solutions it chooses to certain problems which reveal themselves as dilemmas" (p. 8). He classifies these problems under the following general headings and subheadings:

A. Relationships with People
   1. Universalism versus Particularism
   2. Individualism versus Communitarianism
   3. Neutral versus Emotional
   4. Specific versus Diffuse
   5. Achievement versus Ascription
B. Attitudes toward Time
C. Attitudes toward Nature and Human Nature

I will briefly discuss these seven items (five relationships and two attitudes) and their possible implications for learning design in various cultures.

Universalism versus Particularism

Universalism (a rules orientation) and particularism (a relationship orientation) strongly influence the thinking of managers and employees in different cultures.

Universalist cultures adhere to standards that are universally agreed upon by the culture. Universalist, or rule-based cultures, have a tendency to resist exceptions. Trompenaars (1998, p. 31) gives the example of crossing the street when the traffic light is red. You will be frowned at in rule-based societies, like France or Germany, if you cross the street with a red light late at night, even if there are no cars in sight. Particularists, in contrast, focus on the nature of the particular situation, no matter what the rules say.

"Business people from both societies will tend to think each other corrupt" (Trompenaars, 1998, p.31). The universalists believe the particularists cannot be trusted because "they don't follow the rules." Particularists don't trust universalists because "they won't even help a friend in need because of rules."

Individualism versus Communitarianism

Individualism (emphasis on the individual) and communitarianism (emphasis on the group) obviously influence a culture's expectations for managers and employees. Certain practices, such as pay-for-performance and achievement-based promotions, work well in individualistic cultures but are typically unsuccessful in communitarian societies.

In individualistic cultures, organizations are created to serve the needs of individuals. In communitarian societies, organizations are seen as large families, communities, or clans, to which members contribute and in which they all share.

Neutral versus Emotional

Trompenaars (1998, p. 73) believes, "The amount of emoting is a major difference between cultures." Expecting managers or employees to express or control emotions from one cultural setting to another is quite important. An emotional outburst (defined differently in different cultures) can be seen as the high-level commitment of a dedicated manager or as the ravings of an unprofessional incompetent.

Specific versus Diffuse

How far should a manager get involved with his or her subordinates' personal lives? "Specific" societies believe employers/managers should discuss only job-related matters with workers. "Diffuse" cultures believe a manager is cold if he or she doesn't express an interest in a worker's personal life. Knowing the boundary between public and private space for employees in a particular society is very important.

Achievement versus Ascription

Trompenaars (1998) correctly states, "All societies give certain of their members higher status than others" (p. 105). Everybody agrees with that assertion. The critical question here is: How do they determine whom to give the higher status to?

"Achievement" societies give status based on accomplishments (e.g., degrees earned, money earned, "winning"). "Ascriptive" cultures give status based on who you are (e.g., family membership, gender, age). In some ascriptive societies, a high-achievement manager may never be highly respected because it is believed his or her family membership, gender, or age (regardless of accomplishments) doesn't warrant high status.

Attitudes toward Time

Cultures can be categorized as present-oriented, past-oriented, or future-oriented. Present-oriented cultures are basically traditionless and ignore the future. Past-oriented societies are concerned about maintaining traditions. Future-oriented societies envision a different and more desirable future (Trompenaars, 1998, p. 124).

Trompenaars (1998) believes, "How we think of time is interwoven with how we plan, strategize, and coordinate our activities with others" (p. 124). Therefore, every activity of an employee is affected by his or her time orientation.

Trompenaars also distinguishes between sequential cultures and synchronic cultures. "Sequential" cultures tend to schedule very tightly; "time is money" to the sequential society members. "Synchronic" cultures are less punctual or time-conscious; their members believe you should give time to people (Trompenaars, 1998, p. 128).

Beliefs about time greatly influence our management practices and expectations about employees. By their nature, strategic planning and goal setting require a future orientation.

Attitudes toward Nature & Human Nature

Can we control nature? Or does nature control us? Julian Rotter attempted to measure how people think about these two questions. Rotter (1966) distinguished between people with an internal locus of control and people with an external locus of control. The ancient Greeks believed virtue was to achieve "harmonia," living in harmony with the natural forces of the world.

The modern Western mind, especially in the American "rags-to-riches" mindset, is driven by an internal locus of control. Western corporations clearly seek managers with an internal locus of control.

IMPLICATIONS FOR CROSS-CULTURAL DESIGN

Let's look at five geographical areas (U.S., Germany, Mexico, the Arab countries, and Japan) in an attempt to better understand the implications of Hofstede and Trompenaars' work. Hofstede (1993) reports the following (100 is the high end of his scales):

	US	GER	MX	ARAB	JP
Power Distance	40	35	81	80	54
Individuality	91	67	30	38	46
Uncertainty Avoidance	46	35	82	68	92
Masculinity	62	66	69	53	95

There are some obvious similarities between the U.S. and German numbers (except for the almost comical 91 on U.S. individualism). There are also some interesting similarities between Mexico and the Arab countries. Japan seems to be in a category of its own with extremely high scores on uncertainty avoidance and masculinity.

Trompenaars' 1998 work reveals additional differences on several continua. Companies in Japan, Mexico, and Germany are relationship-oriented (the company is a "group of people"). Companies in the U.S. and the Arab countries are task-oriented (the company is a "system" to complete a task).

On the universalism versus particularism dimension, the U.S. and Germany were strongly universalistic. Mexico and Japan were mildly particularistic. The Arab countries were not ranked on this dimension.

On individual freedom the U.S. scored very high, while Germany was moderate (53 on a scale of 100). Mexico, Japan, and the Arab countries scored low on individual freedom. On the importance of receiving individual credit, the U.S. scored very high; Germany scored moderately high. Mexico, Japan, and the Arab countries scored low.

Expressing feelings on the job is fine in the Arab countries; it is taboo in Japan. The other countries fall in between. The degree to which a manager should get involved with an employee's personal life varies greatly. In communist (and former communist) countries, it is expected. In Japan and the Arab countries it is permissible in some cases. In Germany and the U.S. it is typically seen unfavorably.

Looking at the ways in which cultures accord status reveals dramatic differences in cultural assumptions. The U.S. is highly achievement-based. Mexico, Japan, and Germany are moderately achievement-based. The Arab countries are highly ascription-based.

The efficient use of time was very important in Germany and the U.S.; it was less important in Mexico. Beliefs about nature and human nature varied dramatically. Americans saw themselves as "masters of their fates." The Arab countries viewed the American belief skeptically. Germany and Japan were moderate on whom or what controls their lives.

These last two dimensions greatly influence strategic planning, goal setting, and the general expectations for managers. Additionally, Trompenaars looked at what degree of supervision should be given to employees as they do their jobs. In the Arab countries high degrees of supervision were seen as necessary (what Americans call "micro-managing"). In Germany and the U.S., employees were left alone to do their jobs.

All of these differences in cultural expectations must be considered in any cross-cultural training and development effort.

REFERENCE

Beitler, M.A. (1999). Learning and development agreements for mid-career professionals. *Performance in Practice*, Fall 1999, American Society for Training and Development.

Beitler, M.A.(2000). The role of contract learning in the learning organization. *HR.com*, September, 2000.

Beitler, M.A. & Frady, D.A. (2002). E-learning and E-support for expatriate managers. In H.B. Long & Associates, *Self-directed learning in the information age*. Schaumberg, IL: Motorola University Press.

Bennett, J.M. (1986). Modes of cross-cultural training: Conceptualizing cross-cultural training as education. *International Journal of Intercultural Relations*, 10, 117–134.

Bhawuk, D.P.S. & Brislin, R. (1992). The measurement of intercultural sensitivity using the concepts of individualism and collectivism. *International Journal of Intercultural Relations*, 16, 413–436.

Black, J.S. & Gregersen, H. B. (1999). The right way to manage expats. *Harvard Business Review*, March-April, 53.

Copeland, L. & Griggs, L. (1985). *Going international*. New York: Plume.

Dallas, S. (1995). Rule No. 1: Don't diss the locals. *Business Week*, May 15, 117–26.

Farley, P. (1987). Intercultural training for managers: A comparison of documentary and interpersonal methods. *Academy of Management Journal*, 30, 685–698.

Harris, P.R. & Moran, R.T. (1991). *Managing cultural differences*. Houston, TX: Gulf Publishing.

Harrison, J.K. (1992). The individual and combined effects of behavior modeling and the cultural assimilator in cross-cultural management training. *Journal of Applied Psychology*, 77(6), 952–962.

Harrison, J.K. (1994). Developing successful expatriate managers: A framework for the structural design and strategic alignment of cross-cultural training programs. *Human Resource Planning*, September, v.17, n.3, 17–36.

Hofstede, G. (1980). *Culture's consequences.* Beverly Hills, CA: Sage Publications.

Hofstede, G. (1993). Cultural constraints in management theories. *Academy of Management Executive*, 7(1), 81–94.

Hogan, G.W. & Goodson, J.R. (1990). The key to expatriate success. *Training & Development Journal*, January, 50–53.

Jordan, J. & Cartwright, S. (1998). Selecting expatriate managers: Key traits and competencies. *Leadership & Organizational Development Journal*, March-April, vol. 19, 89–97.

Kelley, C. & Meyers, J.E. (1992). *The cross-cultural adaptability inventory.* Yarmouth, ME: Intercultural Press.

Kluckhohn, F. & Strodtbeck, F.L. (1961). *Variations in value orientations.* Evanston, IL: Row, Peterson.

Mendenhall, M. & Oddou, G. (1985). The dimensions of expatriate acculturation: A review. *Academy of Management Review*, 10(1), 39–47.

Oechsler, W.A. (1999). Global management and local systems of employment relations. In J. Engelhard & W. A. Oechsler (Eds.), *Internationales Management.* Wiesbaden, Germany: Gabler.

Rotter, J. (1966). Generalized expectancies for internal versus external control of reinforcements, *Psychological Monographs*, 80, Whole No. 609.

Trompenaars, F. (1998). *Riding the waves of culture: Understanding diversity in global business* (2nd ed.). New York: McGraw-Hill.

Tung, R. (1981). Selection and training of personnel for overseas assignments. *Columbia Journal of World Business*, Spring, 68–78.

CHAPTER 8

Corporate Universities

Every OL consultant, training director, and senior executive should stay abreast of the current developments at corporate universities. There are more than 1,000 corporate universities in operation.

Corporate universities can do more than provide employee learning opportunities; they can provide a strategic competitive advantage. Karen Neely Jones, founding dean of Oracle University, said, "We realize that the skills and knowledge of Oracle's employees and partners are as strategic an asset as the products and services we offer."

In this chapter we will discuss the following corporate university (CU) issues:

1. The CU model
2. Designing a CU
3. Developing External Learning Partnerships
4. Partnering with Traditional Universities
5. Possible Structures and Scope

THE CU MODEL

It is impossible to talk about "the" CU model. Some CUs have a well-equipped campus (e.g., GE and Motorola); some CUs have no campus at all (e.g., Dell and Sun Microsystems).

Some CUs focus on the developmental needs of middle and senior management. According to Louise Korver, Director of Leadership Education at Ingersoll-Rand's corporate university, IR University focuses on the needs of the organization's top 2,500 leaders.

Other CUs offer a wide range of structured programs and courses for all organizational members. Nancy Ford, Senior Internal Consultant at North Carolina Baptist Hospitals' Leadership Academy, says the NCBH Leadership Academy offers courses and programs for organizational members from staff-level employees to executives.

Every CU must be designed to support the organization's clearly defined purpose and strategic plan. Therefore, every CU is (and should be) designed differently. We will look more closely at design in the second section of this chapter.

Jeanne Meister, a leading authority on corporate universities, believes the corporate university can provide "The strategic umbrella for developing and educating employees, customers, and suppliers in order to meet an organization's business strategies" (1998, p. 29).

CUs can go far beyond the traditional training department model of providing training workshops for the company's employees. In addition to the company's employees, CUs can provide learning opportunities for the company's entire value chain. The value chain includes customers, suppliers, dealers, distributors, and even traditional educational institutions.

Educational institutions, including vocational/technical schools and universities, are wisely included in some CU value chain considerations because these institutions supply human capital for the organization. Every company has a stake in the quality of our educational institutions' "products" (the graduates). As a stakeholder, the company and its CU are behooved to be actively engaged in the educational system.

"Just as each state relies on some form of the traditional university model to systematize higher education and avoid unnecessary duplication, companies with corporate universities employ the university model to organize their learning and development experiences into one cohesive, purposeful whole" (Meister, 1998, p. 30).

When it is aligned with the company's mission and strategic plan, the CU is a powerful way to organize and streamline learning efforts.

Meister's Ten Goals & Principles

Jeanne Meister offers ten goals and principles for CUs in her widely used book, *Corporate Universities* (1998, pp. 30–31):

1. "Provide learning opportunities that support the organization's critical business issues.
2. "Consider the corporate university model a process rather than a place of learning.
3. "Design a curriculum to incorporate the three Cs: corporate citizenship, contextual framework, and core competencies.
4. "Train the value chain, including customers, distributors, product suppliers, and the universities that provide tomorrow's workers.
5. "Move from instructor-led training to multiple formats of delivering learning.
6. "Encourage leaders to be involved with, and to facilitate, learning.
7. "Move from a corporate allocation funding model to one 'self-funded' by the business units (the users).
8. "Assume a global focus in developing learning solutions.
9. "Create a measurement system to evaluate outputs as well as inputs.
10. "Utilize the corporate university for competitive advantage and entry into new markets."

Every company with a new CU, or established CU, should follow Meister's guidance. Otherwise, the CU will eventually degenerate into an over-funded training department.

DESIGNING A CU

Designing a CU is a critical step. If the CU is not aligned with the organization's mission, or if it does not contribute to the implementation of the company's strategic plan, it does little more than generate large expenditures.

An analysis of the company's strategic plan should lead to a discussion about required KSAs (knowledge, skills, and attitudes) for successful implementation of the strategic plan. This discussion may lead to the possibility of establishing a CU. But as Jeanne Meister said, the CU serves only as the "umbrella" for all organizational learning activities. The design of what's under the umbrella will require a large contribution of people, time, and resources.

CU design requires the rigorous processes of determining learning needs, identifying learning resources, and creating knowledge management systems to capture and disseminate learning. Completing these critical processes is best facilitated by an outside OL consultant.

Learning should be seen as a strategy for establishing and maintaining competitive advantage. But like any other sustainable competitive advantage, this strategy requires high-level organizational support and leadership.

Meister's Design Guidance

There are many questions to answer during the design phase. Meister (1998, pp. 65–85) offers detailed guidance. I will attempt to briefly summarize her comments here.

1. Determine Appropriate Governance & Leadership's Role:
   Is there strong visible support from the top?
   Is there a coalition of managers to give the effort a critical mass in its early stages?
   Should there be centralized administration and measurement?
2. Create a Vision:
   Is there a vision that makes a lasting impression on all key stakeholders?
3. Recommend Scope & Funding Strategy:
   Which employees and customer/supply chain stakeholders will be served?
   How will the CU be funded? Annual budget allocation or through chargebacks to business unit users?

4. Create an Organization:
   Which functions will be centralized?
   Which functions will be decentralized?
5. Identify Interests/Concerns of Stakeholders:
   What are the interests of each stakeholder group?
6. Create Products and Services:
   What learning solutions will be offered?
   How will self-directed learning be supported?
   Will subject matter experts (SMEs) be made available?
   Will learning consultants be made available?
7. Select Learning Partners:
   Which vendors, consultants, and institutions of higher learning will serve as partners?
   Will college credit or other rewards be offered?
8. Draft a Technology Strategy:
   What role will technology play?
   What learner-controlled products will be available?
9. Create an Evaluation System:
   Are learning objectives being fulfilled?
   Is learning contributing to business needs?
   How will performance improvement be measured?
10. Communicate:
    How will the role of the CU be communicated?
    How will frequently asked questions be addressed?
    How will CU successes be communicated?

Designing the CLO Position

There is one more design issue to consider. The position of Chief Learning Officer (CLO) must be designed around four key roles: business partner, systems thinker, senior education officer, and alliance builder.

As business partner, the CLO must understand "the company's strategic direction, its products, services, customers, competitors, suppliers, union issues, and how the organization is positioning itself in the global marketplace" (Meister, 1998, p. 86).

As systems thinker, the CLO must see how the organizational learning activities are linked to the strategic objectives. All parts of the CU must operate as a unified whole.

The CLO is the organization's senior education officer. As the organization's senior learning consultant, the CLO must have more than training "platform skills." The CLO must have business savvy, leadership skills, and vision, as well as the knowledge contained in this book.

Finally, the role of alliance builder cannot be over-emphasized. The CLO must form alliances and partnerships with senior line and staff managers, union leaders, customers, suppliers, independent trainers, and deans of university business schools. CLOs of global companies must develop and maintain a global network of learning partners.

In the next section, we will discuss the role of alliance/ partnership builder in more detail.

DEVELOPING EXTERNAL LEARNING PARTNERSHIPS

The concept of the CU as an "umbrella" for organizational learning activities must be clear to senior management. The CU is not an attempt to do everything "in-house." As the coordinator of all organizational learning activities, rather than the "provider" of all organizational activities, the CU is free to utilize external resources as well as internal resources to address learning needs.

Partnering with Independent Vendors

CU partnering with independent training vendors goes far beyond what traditional training departments have called "outsourced training." While many traditional T&D departments utilize independent vendors for one-time or specialized training, many CUs forge long-term, mutually beneficial partnerships with independent vendors.

As we all know, partnerships succeed long term only if both parties benefit, so this arrangement is not simply a matter of negotiating for the lowest price on a single training event. Forging long-term partnerships involves creating a shared vision, developing a strategic plan, and clarifying expectations about implementing the plan. This process is hard work that requires a commitment of time and effort.

Building these alliances and partnerships greatly increases the value of the CU to the organization. Creating and maintaining these relationships substantially increase the availability of learning opportunities for organizational members.

The list of possible external vendors for learning includes training companies, consulting firms, independent trainers, professional societies and associations, and traditional universities. (Later in this chapter, we will look at some creative alliances between CUs and traditional universities.) These external vendors have specialized knowledge and/or facilities. It is not efficient or cost-effective for the CU to attempt to duplicate resources that are already available. Hence, partnerships are the answer.

Partnering with Value Chain Members

CU partnering with value chain members (suppliers, dealers, distributors, and customers) is more than a good learning strategy. It's good business. Building relationships is critical in an age when achieving tangible product differentiation is nearly impossible. American companies are trying to catch up with the rest of the world on this concept of building relationships to build business.

Partnering with value chain members helps to establish a common set of quality standards. Value chain members learn the company's expectations through the various learning opportunities offered by the CU.

Some companies, such as Lord Corporation (a diversified technology-based company), have gone so far as to acquire state licensure for its CU programs. Lord Institute offers certificate and degree programs for its suppliers and distributors. State licensure adds credibility and value.

Harley-Davidson University offers formal courses and a self-study library to its domestic and international dealers and distributors. Motorola University goes beyond its value chain to offer learning opportunities, for a fee, to any organization interested in its programs.

As you can see, CUs offer more than education. CUs can serve a critical role in building strategic relationships.

Partnering with Traditional Universities

Partnerships between CUs and traditional universities (TUs) have become very creative. In this section, we will look at some of the ways to benefit from these partnerships.

The Herculean task of preparing the workforce with basic knowledge and skills, and then providing continuous updating of practitioner knowledge and skills, should be shared by the society as a whole. Everybody has a stake in this process. Corporations cannot bear the full responsibility.

Most societies throughout history have recognized the importance of a partnership between parents and teachers. Parent-teacher organizations were born to support those partnerships.

Most societies today are attempting to educate everybody to at least a minimum level. But minimum skills are not sufficient to succeed in a highly competitive, knowledge-driven economy. The various stakeholders must work together to fulfill society's learning needs.

Best of Both Worlds

Alliances between CUs and TUs can offer the best of two different worlds. "Pure" research and general knowledge and skills are still best conducted and delivered by TUs; "applied" research and company-specific knowledge and skills clearly need the involvement of the CU. For efficiency (and effectiveness), "pure" research should be funded by CUs and conducted by TUs. All stakeholders, including individuals and society as a whole, benefit from these CU/TU partnerships.

According to Barbara Thomas, Jan Gilchrist, and Chris Bennett of Blue University, partnerships with traditional universities provide valuable benefits. They believe Blue Cross/Blue Shield of North Carolina, its employees, and, ultimately, its customers benefit from Blue University's partnerships with colleges and universities that offer certificate and licensure programs, undergraduate degrees, and graduate degrees. These partnerships with traditional universities lead to higher levels of employee satisfaction and retention. These partnerships also allow Blue University's professional staff to focus on insurance industry-specific and company-specific competencies.

Another example is Whirlpool Corporation and its TU partners. Whirlpool has developed TU partnerships internationally and domestically. Its international partner is INSEAD in France; its American partners are Indiana University and the University of Michigan. INSEAD has helped educate senior Whirlpool managers on how to deal effectively with joint venture agreements in Asia. Whirlpool serves as a great example of utilizing existing expertise domestically and internationally.

Customized Programs

"Generic programs are becoming less appropriate as corporations demand executive development programs that support their strategic objectives and reflect their vision" (Meister, 1998, p.190). David Sprague, director of the Center for Professional Excellence at Central Michigan University's College of Extended Learning, believes customized programs will replace many of the tuition-reimbursement approaches currently utilized by many companies. This new model requires active participation, rather than passive funding, by corporate management.

Many customized CU/TU-partnership programs now exist for individual companies in which specific degree programs are taught on-site at the corporation's facilities. Other CU/TU-developed degree programs have been developed for entire industries.

Two specific examples of customized programs for entire industries include the T. Eaton Company/Ryerson Polytechnic University program in Canada and the Megatech Engineering/Central Michigan University program in the U.S.

The Eaton School of Retailing was developed by T. Eaton Company, a large Canadian retailer, and Ryerson Polytechnic University to serve the learning needs of retailers. Initially, a retail management certificate was offered to Eaton's employees and to Eaton's suppliers. But the long-range plan was to offer a retailing degree program to all retailers through a distance learning program with Bell Canada.

Megatech Engineering, a Michigan-based automotive design company, envisioned a program that would produce highly skilled designers for the automotive industry. Together with Central Michigan University, Megatech's vision will improve the pool of designers for an entire industry. Companies wishing to be industry leaders should consider initiating similar partnerships.

The Multi-Company Consortium

A hybrid between the open enrollment program offered by TUs and customized CU/TU programs is the multi-company consortium. In the consortium arrangement, companies with similar needs form an alliance with a TU to design programs to meet the learning needs of the consortium members.

Southern Company, an Atlanta-based company, initiated the creation of a consortium of 12 local companies that works with Emory University to deliver programs in executive development and leadership skills. The consortium designed a high-quality, three-week learning experience spread over a three-month period.

The Global Wireless Education Consortium (GWEC) includes Ericsson, Motorola, AT&T Wireless, and Lucent Technologies. GWEC was founded in 1996 to address the acute shortage of technicians and engineers in the industry. GWEC partnered with both a technical college and the University of Texas. The individual companies, the industry's customers, and the future of the industry will be the beneficiaries of this consortium.

POSSIBLE STRUCTURES AND SCOPE

The possibilities for corporate universities are limitless. In this section, I would like to share with you a sampling of the possible structures and scopes for CUs. Many of these examples are based upon my interviews with CU managers ("deans").

Many CUs are structured like a traditional university business school, with a manager ("dean") and various department heads. In a traditional university business school structure, you will find department heads over marketing, management, finance, and HR, all reporting to the business school dean.

In the corporate university structure you may not find the title of "dean," but you will find a CU manager serving as the administrative chief. The responsibilities of the individual department heads vary greatly, depending on the CU's mission statement.

Carla Fox, Senior Vice President and Manager of BB&T University, oversees eight departments. But at BB&T University you will not find the traditional business school departments previously named. Instead, you will find departments such as Credit Training, Operations Training, Process Improvement, Professional Development, and University Administration & Technology. The scope of BB&T University is quite broad. Under the BB&T University umbrella you will also find executive coaching, counseling, and the career profiling system. The University is staffed with more than 100 full-time employees.

Trilogy's Boot Camp

In a fascinating article by Noel Tichy published in *Harvard Business Review on Developing Leaders* in 2004 (originally published as a *Harvard Business Review* article in 2001), Tichy described Trilogy's "boot camp," a comprehensive orientation program for new hires. At Trilogy, a corporate boot camp is much more than a new-hire orientation program.

We have all heard of corporate boot camps. Some of the best boot camps, including GE's and Ford's, put new hires to work on real business problems immediately, so action learning at corporate boot camps is not new. It is also not new to get CEO and senior executive involvement; we have all heard about the stories of Watson at IBM, Perot at EDS, and Grove at Intel.

Trilogy University is unique in that it serves as the "primary R&D engine" and "incubator for Trilogy's strategic thinking" (Tichy, 2004, p. 64). Trilogy's boot camp is intense and intimidating, and it lasts for three months. After a month of orientation in cohorts of 20, recruits begin developing "frame-breaking" new business ideas in month two. In teams of three to five, the recruits:

1. come up with an idea
2. create a business model
3. build the prototype
4. develop the marketing plan

This process is not hypothetical; it's the real thing. The CEO and senior executives play the role of venture capitalists. Approximately 15 percent of the projects survive this stage.

In month three, the recruits are evaluated on various abilities. According to Allan Drummond, Vice President and Manager of Trilogy University, "We don't just want understanding; we want agreement." This agreement on abilities is essential before determining career objectives at Trilogy.

Also in month three, recruits seek a sponsor in the company. You don't graduate from Trilogy's boot camp until you find a manager who will make a commitment to help your career.

Trilogy provides a great example of maximizing the benefits of its corporate university. Trilogy's strategy and culture require customer-focused, risk-taking professionals who work well in teams. Trilogy University is designed to provide the human capital necessary to fulfill Trilogy's mission and strategy plan.

REFERENCES

Beitler, M.A. (2003). *Strategic Organizational Change*. Greensboro, NC: Practitioner Press International.

Meister, J.C. (1998). *Corporate Universities*, (rev. ed.) New York: McGraw-Hill.

Tichy, N.M. (2004). No ordinary boot camp. Chapter in *Harvard Business Review on Developing Leaders*. Boston, MA: Harvard Business School Publishing.

CHAPTER 9

Consulting Skills

Throughout this book, I have offered many opportunities for OL consultants to grow as strategic partners in the service of their clients. The opportunities for OL consultants are as varied as "specializing" in expatriate development to "generalizing" in the planning and maintaining of corporate universities.

The key for consultant success is to add value to the client organization. Building the consultant-client relationship is critical.

In this chapter, we will look at some of the prerequisite skills for OL consulting success. I cannot over-emphasize the importance of these skills. Time spent reading the literature on consulting skills is time well spent. Let's begin our discussion with an overview of Process Consulting.

Process Consulting

For many years, I have given Process Consulting workshops for consultants (internal and external). Edgar Schein developed Process Consulting for "helpers." The subtitle of Schein's (1999) book is *Building the Helping Relationship.*

Everyone at various times serves as a helper. Consultants, teachers, trainers, managers, IT and HR professionals, even police officers, find themselves in the role of helper. I have given workshops for all of these groups (and more). All of my workshop attendees can immediately see how to apply Process Consulting in their work.

In this chapter, we will take a brief look at how OL consultants can benefit from Process Consulting skills. (For a more detailed discussion, see Beitler, 2003 or Schein, 1999.)

Three Consulting Approaches

Schein (1999) believes there are basically three approaches to helping: the expert model, the doctor-patient model, and the process consultation model.

In the expert model, the client diagnoses the problem and then purchases the expertise of a consultant. This method is appropriate in some situations. If a company determines it needs an intranet system to enhance its in-house communications, it should purchase the expertise of an IT consultant (based on its own diagnosis).

But the appropriate use of the expert model is based on several assumptions, including:

1. The *client* can properly diagnose the problem.
2. The client can properly communicate the relevant facts to the consultant.

The doctor-patient (or physician) model also has appropriate and inappropriate applications. In this model, the patient/client simply describes symptoms. Then the physician/consultant diagnoses the problem and decides on a solution. This model may be appropriate (in some cases required) when the patient/client has little or no knowledge to contribute to the physician/ consultant's decision.

But the appropriate use of the physician model is also based on certain assumptions, including:

1. The *consultant* can properly diagnose the problem.
2. The client can properly communicate the relevant facts to the consultant.

The third model, developed and advocated by Schein, is Process Consultation. In the Process Consulting model, the consultant immediately involves the client as a partner. The consultant and client collaboratively diagnose the problem, design and implement interventions, and evaluate the success of the interventions.

Schein (1999) lists several guidelines for consultant success with the Process Consulting model:

1. The consultant must communicate that the client "owns" the problem.
2. The consultant and client (e.g., line manager) must work together as equal partners.
3. The client knows what will and will not work in its culture, so client participation and "buy-in" are essential.

The Process Consulting model offers several advantages for the consultant:

1. The consultant does *not* have to be a content (e.g., marketing, production, logistics, finance) expert to be helpful.
2. The consultant does *not* have to decide what the client must do. The consultant facilitates the client's decision-making process.
3. The client's valuable input is available throughout the process.

The Psychodynamics of Helping

In any helping relationship, there are several possible reactions by the helper (consultant) and the helped (client). Unfortunately, many of these reactions are highly destructive to the effectiveness of the relationship.

The possible negative reactions of the client include resentment and defensiveness or relief and dependency. Resentment and defensiveness lead the client to look for opportunities to make the consultant look bad. The client may challenge and resist all of the consultant's input.

The client may also react with relief and dependency. Relief is usually expressed verbally as, "I'm so glad you're here." Then the client drops a stack of file folders in the consultant's lap and runs down the hallway. Dependency is expressed by a client helplessly saying, "I don't have any ideas, you are the expert."

Schein (1999) warns consultants about the "Power Vacuum." The power vacuum is how Schein illustrates the possibility of the consultant getting "sucked in" to taking responsibility for the client's problem.

These destructive client reactions are often exacerbated by the consultant's emotional reactions. Client defensiveness is often met with consultant defensiveness and additional pressure to agree with him or her. I once heard a consultant condescendingly say, "I don't think you understood my suggestion; let me explain it in a simpler way that you can understand."

Consultants are often guilty of accepting and encouraging client dependency. Comments like, "Don't you worry about it, I'll take care of everything," foster client dependency. Frankly, some consultants enjoy the power and authority that is ascribed to the expert.

Other issues to keep in mind here are transference and countertransference (please excuse the Freudian terminology). Transference involves the client's perceiving the consultant as a parent, school teacher, or some past negative authority figure. Countertransference involves the consultant's perceiving the client as a past negative client.

It is important that the consultant remain aware of the current psychodynamics occurring between him/herself and the client. It is essential that a collaborative and cooperative relationship be established and maintained.

All the Things You Don't Know

Perhaps the strangest sounding, but most helpful, of Schein's advice is to write down "all the things you don't know" (1999, p. 41). That's right—don't know! As consultants or helpers we are accustomed to writing down everything we do know. But according to Schein, this habit can get the "process" consultant into trouble. By only writing down what he or she knows, the consultant may make a premature recommendation.

This idea of Schein's has saved me on many occasions. As a consultant, I frequently feel time pressure from the client, who is paying by the hour and understandably concerned about time and, ultimately, fees.

Time pressure on the client leads to time pressure on the consultant. The consultant is subtly (and often not so subtly) pressured for quick solutions to problems. It is not uncommon for a client to offer a few sketchy details, and then ask expectantly, "What do you think?" In this situation the consultant runs the risk of making a big mistake: a premature, ill-prepared recommendation.

By writing down all the things I *don't* know, I can slow down the process. Both parties benefit from my "don't know list":

1. I, the consultant, can clearly see that I don't have enough information to make a recommendation.
2. The client clearly sees that the consultant has legitimate questions about the situation. Frequently, the client realizes that he or she has not even considered these questions.

By writing down all the things we don't know, we take the focus off time and place it on building a collaborative working relationship.

Active Inquiry

An essential part of Schein's Process Consulting practice model is the use of Active Inquiry. A guiding assumption in Active Inquiry is that an insecure client will not reveal essential facts about the organization's situation. Without these essential facts, the consultant is placed in a position of guessing. The consultant is then forced to rely on the dubious practice of projecting his or her prior experiences into the client's current situation.

Schein describes three levels of Active Inquiry: pure inquiry, exploratory/diagnostic inquiry, and confrontive inquiry. It is important for the consultant to use the appropriate level at particular points in the process. The type of data being sought should determine the level of inquiry.

Pure inquiry, the first level, is designed to stimulate full disclosure. The consultant is simply attempting to get the story in as factual a manner as possible. At this level, "who" and "when" questions are appropriate; "why" questions are not.

Exploratory/diagnostic inquiry, the second level, is appropriate after the whole "factual" story is recorded. The consultant now redirects the client's focus with questions such as:

"How did you feel about that?"

"Why do you suppose he/she did that?"

"What are you going to do next?"

Exploratory/diagnostic inquiry gets the client to explore at a deeper level. At this level, feelings, hypotheses, cause and effect relationships, and forecasted actions can be discussed. This level reveals organizational and client member expectations, perceptions, and values.

Confrontive (not "confrontational") inquiry, the third level, must not occur before completing pure inquiry or exploratory/diagnostic inquiry. At this level, the consultant interjects his/her ideas about the situation. The goal here is to move the client members from unproductive thinking to creative and critical thinking about the current situation.

Face Work

In building an effective relationship with the client, Schein (1999) recommends the use of "face work" (pp. 109–116). The concept of "saving face" originated in Asian societies, but it is applicable in learning and change interventions throughout the world.

Frequently, a client feels "one down" when a consultant is hired. The client may feel that the hiring of the consultant indicates his or her inability to deal with a problem. This sense of inadequacy (feeling "one down") on the part of the client must be quickly overcome in order to establish a collaborative working relationship.

At the beginning of an engagement, a client with "exposed face" will have difficulty being open and honest with the consultant. Fear of humiliation will motivate defensive behavior.

In this situation, the consultant must "grant face" to the client:

1. Assure the client that his or her input is essential to the success of an intervention. (The client is the "content" expert).
2. Assure the client that it's common for organizations to have such problems.
3. Share successes of similar organizations with similar problems.

As long as the client feels one down, the consultant cannot work effectively. Frequently, clients do not reveal the real problem at first because of embarrassment. It is difficult for client members to discuss their perceived failures with a complete stranger. Consultants must earn their clients' trust.

Summary of Process Consulting

The goal of Process Consulting is to build an open and honest relationship, in which both facts and feelings can be shared. The client has essential information about the organization and the "problem."

An essential aspect of Process Consulting is status equilibration. The advantages of building a relationship of equal partners include:

1. Diagnostic insights make sense to both the consultant and the client because they are speaking the same language.
2. Solutions, in the form of interventions, are realistic for the organization's culture.
3. Evaluations of the outcomes are based on objectives that were jointly determined by the consultant and the client.

PERFORMANCE CONSULTING

Organizational learning (OL) consultants, trainers, and managers should be aware of the performance consulting movement. Performance consulting has been widely embraced by trainers and the ASTD (American Society for Training & Development) since the 1990s. Many ASTD members are also members of the ISPI (International Society for Performance Improvement).

Performance consultants advocate a change of focus from training to performance improvement. An ASTD survey of more than

300 senior managers and executives in 1998 identified ten probable trends in training. A "shift from providing training to improving performance" was ranked the most probable trend within the next few years. That prediction seems to be right on target.

Robinson and Robinson (1998) summarized the "new" goal of the training or HRD (human resource development) departments as follows: "to enhance human performance in support of business goals" (p. 3). This approach requires the alignment of four types of needs:

- business needs
- performance needs
- learning needs
- work environment needs

Judith Robb (1998) expounds on these four needs. She defines business needs as the operational or strategic goals of the unit, department, or organization. "Performance needs describe what people need to do to meet the operational goals" (p. 232). She sees learning needs as the required skills and knowledge to perform successfully. Finally, she describes work environment needs as "the systems, tools, and processes required if the performance needs are to be achieved" (p. 232).

Robb (1998) goes on to say, "The client's business goals should be part of every decision" (p. 233). She is in complete agreement with my belief that everything in the organization should be driven by the strategic plan. Success or failure of any initiative should be determined by desired business results.

The Practice Model

Performance consultants follow a four-phase practice model strikingly similar to the four-phase model of traditional training (see Figure 9.1 below).

Four-Phase Models

Performance Consulting	Traditional Training
Partnering	Assessing (TNA)
Assessing	Designing
Implementing	Conducting
Measuring	Evaluating

FIGURE 9.1 Four-Phase Models

The difference is a philosophical one. Performance consultants reject the order-taking role to which traditional trainers have been relegated.

When the traditional trainer receives a client call, he or she begins the assessing phase by conducting a training needs analysis (TNA). The problem with this approach, according to the performance consultants, is that it presumes there is a training problem and a training solution. I agree; this presumption could be misleading.

Partnering Phase

Partnering, according to Geoffrey Bellman (1998), is essential to success whenever people are working together. It is important during this first phase to define "success." What would successful results look like?

Contracting between the client and consultant is a critical part of the partnering phase. Bellman (1998) states, "A contract is 'the deal' within which people play out their relationship. It is about what we each are willing to give and what we want in return" (p. 43). It is worth the time it takes to make these expectations explicit.

Bellman (1998) insightfully adds, "Some form of contract is always there, whether discussed or not, whether mutually understood or not . . ." (p. 43).

The literature on partnering for performance consultants is similar to, and in agreement with, the relationship building advocated by Schein (1999) in his Process Consulting Model. (For more on this, see Beitler, 2003, chapter 3.)

Assessing Phase

The assessing phase in performance consulting is different from the assessing phase in traditional training. In the traditional training model, a training need is assumed. Not so in the performance consulting model.

Similar to the traditional training model, assessing in the performance consulting model is used as the basis for designing interventions, which may include training. But the goal in this model is to enhance performance, not merely knowledge.

Paul Elliott (1998) states, "The focus must be on outputs, which is what workers produce, and not simply on what they do" (p.63). This view of assessing is clearly influenced by Tom Gilbert's (1978) book, entitled *Human Competence*.

This model uses a "gap and cause" analysis. Similar to the traditional training model, a gap and cause analysis contrasts current performance with the organization's expectations.

One significant difference in the assessment phase of the performance consulting model is the use of exemplary performers, individuals whose outputs (results) exceed requirements. Remember, in the traditional training assessment phase the task was to compare current KSAs (knowledge, skills, and attitudes) of the worker with the required KSAs of the job. There can be significant differences between average, successful, and exemplary performers.

Implementing Phase

The implementing phase involves determining the proper intervention(s) and then carrying them out with the client. These interventions are based upon the findings of the assessment phase.

Performance consultants consider both learning and nonlearning interventions. With such a wide range of possible interventions (learning and nonlearning), no single consultant can be an expert in all of them. Stolovitch and Keeps (1998, p. 95) recommend building a "resource bank" of internal and external consultants "to whom work can be brokered when required." They go on to say, "It is unlikely that learning interventions alone will solve complex performance problems" (p. 103).

Nonlearning interventions include everything from reward system changes to improve motivation to environment changes (sometimes simply referred to as "other changes"), such as:

improving information flow,

redesigning jobs,

reducing interruptions,

changing worker selection criteria,

providing technical support.

While the literature on nonlearning interventions tends toward the grandiose, interventions as simple as writing "job aids" are occasionally sufficient. Written job aids are nothing more than task lists, recipes, formulas, or decision tables.

Solovitch and Keeps (1998) recommend systems thinking leading to a "basket of solutions" (p. 113). They point out that outsourcing is not the only option here; another option is "insourcing" (p. 122). The idea of "brokering-in" is not new, but it is often underutilized. Brokering-in involves identifying and using in-house expertise, as discussed in the knowledge capture and transfer chapter (see Chapter 5).

Measuring Phase

Evaluation of performance improvement initiatives (or learning activities) requires an open discussion about desired results and actual results. This step requires a model of "measurements."

Brinkerhoff (1998) offers a five-phase model for evaluation "that parallels the five fundamental errors:"

1. goal setting
2. performance analysis
3. design for improvement
4. implementation
5. impact

Key questions associated with each phase, according to Brinkerhoff (1998), are:

1. "How important and worthwhile is the business goal for the performance improvement project?" (p. 156)
2. "Have sufficient primary performance improvement needs been identified?" (p. 159)
3. "Have correct and sufficient performance improvement methods, tools, and other support aids been identified?" (p. 161)
4. "Were all performer and manager expectations considered and addressed in the design of the performance management tools?" (p. 164)
5. "What evidence is there that performance improvement efforts have 'caused' performance improvements?" (p. 167)

Practitioners in the performance consulting movement place serious emphasis on measuring results. This focus on results should be adopted by all practitioners. Senior executives are increasing the pressure to justify all project expenditures. This is a trend that will not reverse itself.

All consultants, internal and external, whether they call themselves trainers, OL consultants, or performance consultants must provide evidence for their contribution to the organization's business objectives. Understanding of and commitment to the business objectives are essential prerequisites for any consultant hoping to become a strategic business partner.

Summary of Performance Consulting

Performance consulting offers both wisdom and tools for trainers and OL consultants. Judith Hale (1998) believes what "distinguishes performance consultants from other consultants is their lack of bias in terms of finding a solution" (p. 7) While no consultant can be truly bias-free, I believe the intent of her comment is worth considering.

To add more value to organizations, OL consultants must conduct needs analysis to distinguish between learning and nonlearning needs. Thorough needs analysis requires building a strategic partnership with the client and the skillful use of questioning.

OTHER CONSULTING SKILLS

There are two other skill sets consultants should be familiar with: Cooperrider's Appreciative Inquiry and Ellis's A-B-C Model of Perception. Let's start with a brief look at Appreciative Inquiry.

Appreciative Inquiry

A consulting skill that is currently gaining attention is Appreciative Inquiry (AI). The theory and practice of AI is largely driven by the work of David Cooperrider of the Weatherhead School of Management at Case Western Reserve University.

Unfortunately, appreciative inquiry is often painted as a Polyanna-ish approach, in which the consultant and client look only for good things in the situation. But in practice, appreciative inquiry provides a realistic and balanced view of a situation.

Frequently, the consultant enters an organizational atmosphere that is filled with high levels of frustration and perhaps a sense of failure. This negative tone frequently leads to an overly pessimistic viewpoint. Appreciative inquiry helps to balance the negative threats with positive opportunities.

AI focuses on leveraging an organization's strengths, rather than trying to fix or minimize its weaknesses. Based on the idea that organizations move in the direction of what they focus on, AI suggests inquiring into what is going right. Focusing on building upon positives, rather than exclusively focusing on problems, energizes organizational members.

The practice of AI involves re-phrasing questions so that the questions themselves are positive. AI practitioners speak in terms of using an "Asset-Based Approach" (positive view) instead of a "Deficit-Based Approach" (negative view).

AI philosophy is based on the belief that our image of the future drives our action. In others words, positive expectations lead to positive results. Positive expectations generate positive energy.

In my opinion, AI offers us a consulting skill for helping clients maintain a balanced view of their situation. I believe the key is balanced, not overly positive or overly negative.

Ellis's Model of Perception

Albert Ellis is a cognitive psychologist, not a consultant. But, his model of perception is invaluable for us consultants.

A client's belief about an event leads to his or her subsequent thinking or behavior. That may seem obvious, but we frequently "project" our own beliefs and values into the client's situation when we attempt to understand the client's reaction. Big mistake! If we don't understand the client's beliefs, we can't understand the client's reaction.

Ellis and Dryden (1987) reject the S-R (stimulus-response) model of the behavioral psychologists as being overly simplistic for human beings. Ellis offers an A-B-C model:

- A   Activating Event (stimulus)
- B   Belief about the Activating Event
- C   Consequential Thinking and/or Behavior (response)

Ellis is adding the "B" step to the old stimulus-response model. Ellis insists it is the belief about the stimulus (not the stimulus itself) that leads to a particular behavior or thought.

How we (consultants) would react to a certain situation is irrelevant. What is important is how the client perceives the situation, based on his or her values, beliefs, expectations, and assumptions. As consultants we must take the time to understand the bases of our client's thinking and behavior.

REFERENCES

ASTD (1998). "Trends in HRD," *National HRD Executive Survey*. Alexandria, VA: ASTD.

Beitler, M.A. (2003). *Strategic Organizational Change*. Greensboro, NC: Practitioner Press International.

Bellman, G. (1998). Partnership phase: Forming partnerships. In D. Robinson & J. Robinson (Eds.), *Moving from training to performance*. Alexandria, VA: ASTD, and San Francisco: Berrett-Koehler.

Brinkerhoff, R. (1998). Measurement phase: Evaluating effectiveness of performance improvement projects. In D. Robinson & J. Robinson (Eds.), *Moving from training to performance*. Alexandria, VA: ASTD, and San Francisco: Berrett-Koehler.

Cooperrider, D. & Srivastva, S. (1987). Appreciative inquiry in organizational life. In R. Woodman & W. Pasmore (Eds.), *Research in organizational change and development*, Vol.1. Greenwich, CT: JAI Press.

Elliott, P. (1998). Assessment phase: Building models and defining gaps. In D. Robinson & J. Robinson (Eds.), *Moving from training to performance*. Alexandria, VA: ASTD, and San Francisco: Berrett-Koehler.

Ellis, A. & Dryden, W. (1987). *The practice of rational-emotive therapy*. New York: Springer Publishing.

Gilbert, T.F. (1978). *Human competence: Engineering worthy performance*. New York: McGraw-Hill.

Hale, J. (1998). *The performance consultant's fieldbook*. San Francisco: Jossey-Bass/Pfeiffer.

Robb, J. (1998). The job of a performance consultant. In D. Robinson & J. Robinson (Eds.), *Moving from training to performance*. Alexandria, VA: ASTD, and San Francisco: Berrett-Koehler.

Robinson, D.G. & Robinson, J.C. (1998). A focus on performance: What is it? In D. Robinson & J. Robinson (Eds.), *Moving from training to performance*. Alexandria, VA: ASTD, and San Francisco: Berrett-Koehler.

Schein, E.H. (1999). *Process consultation revisited: Building the helping relationship.* Reading, MA: Addison-Wesley.

Stolovitch, H. & Keeps, E. (1998). Implementation phase: performance improvement interventions. In D. Robinson & J. Robinson (Eds.), *Moving from training to performance.* Alexandria, VA: ASTD, and San Francisco: Berrett-Koehler.

CHAPTER 10

The Future of OL

This is an exciting time to be working in the field of organizational learning (OL). Most authorities agree that the era of the traditional trainer patiently waiting for a phone call to deliver a "canned" training program is over.

ASTD, the 70,000-member professional society for workplace learning and performance (WLP) specialists, suggests there is now a great opportunity for WLP professionals to sit at the senior management planning table. The opportunity for a seat at these exclusive planning sessions is rooted in the growing importance of OL. The learning and development of senior management and staff members is critical to organizational success. Tangible assets can no longer provide a sustainable competitive advantage. In the 21st century, people will be the focus for creating and maintaining a sustainable competitive advantage.

While I do not claim to have powers to predict the future, I will make some bold predictions about the future of OL based on the many interviews I did for this book.

TWELVE BOLD PREDICTIONS

1. OL consultants who serve as strategic business partners will rise in status and recognition in organizations. Salaries will rise too as the value of the OL consultant's expertise in learning and performance improvement becomes more widely recognized. (A value-added approach will be critical to fulfilling this prediction.)

2. The role of Chief Learning Officer (CLO) will become commonplace at leading corporations.

3. The field of organization development (OD) will continue to decline in importance for two reasons: (a) many OD practitioners have not adopted a strategic partner approach, and (b) many OD practices have already been adopted by mainstream American businesses.

4. Traditional classroom training will be widely supplemented by self-directed learning (SDL). Many SDL projects will be aided by new technology.

5. Individualized learning agreements will be used more widely as organizations attempt to maximize individual learning efforts.

6. An organization's explicit knowledge will be captured and disseminated (managed) by sophisticated new software. (This software is already in development.) Efficiently codifying explicit knowledge will be critical to an organization's competitiveness.

7. An organization's tacit knowledge will be created and transferred in communities of practice. Leading organizations will recognize that their competitive advantage is in their ability to create and transfer tacit knowledge. Organizations that provide customized products and services will invest heavily in this process.

8. Management and professional development will become more systematized and individualized. In the competitive years ahead, even the best-crafted mission statements and strategic plans will still require extraordinary managers and professional staffs to implement and execute them.

9. A new generation of succession planning will evolve that recognizes changing demographics and facilitates the transfer of power from aging baby-boomers to Gen Xers.

10. Expatriate training and support, especially in American companies, will finally receive the attention (and resources) that it deserves. Organizations will have to be competitive internationally to be competitive at all.

11. The use of corporate universities will continue to grow. (But the corporate universities now functioning as "glorified training departments" will die.) Corporate universities will become the "umbrella" for all organizational learning activities (not just for employees, but for all value chain members and for external as well as internal learning activities).

12. Organizational learning (OL) professionals will be seen as internal learning consultants. The development of consulting skills will enhance the value of OL professionals as strategic business partners.

ASTD's 2004 Competency Study

In ASTD's 2004 "Competency Study" a group of experts developed a professional competency model in the form of a pyramid, including competencies, areas of expertise, and workplace and performance roles.

Competencies

The foundation of the pyramid consists of interpersonal, business/management, and personal competencies.

The required interpersonal competencies include building trust, communicating effectively, influencing stakeholders, leveraging diversity, and networking and partnering.

The business/management competencies (which have been largely undeveloped by traditional trainers) include analyzing needs and proposing solutions, applying business acumen, driving results, planning and implementing assignments, and thinking strategically.

The personal competencies include demonstrating adaptability and modeling personal development.

Areas of Expertise

In the ASTD model, nine areas of expertise are built upon the three types of competencies. The areas of expertise listed by the experts include:

- designing learning
- improving human performance
- delivering training
- measuring and evaluating
- facilitating organizational change
- managing the learning function
- coaching
- managing organizational knowledge
- career planning and talent management

Roles

At the top of the pyramid, the ASTD experts put roles for workplace learning and performance (WLP) professionals. They describe these roles as "broad areas of responsibility" that require "a combination of competencies and areas of expertise" (ASTD, 2004, p.xxiii). They placed roles at the peak of the pyramid because these roles require the support of considerable underlying skills and knowledge.

Three of these roles are of critical importance: business partner, learning strategist, and professional specialist. As a business partner, the WLP professional, or OL consultant, must apply "business and industry knowledge" to help identify workplace performance improvement opportunities. The traditional trainer of years-gone-by would not have thought of this as his or her role.

Another role is that of learning strategist. This role involves "leveraging" learning and performance improvement strategies to "achieve long-term business success" (ASTD, 2004, p.xxiii).

A third role is that of professional specialist. While the acquisition of business and industry knowledge will become more important, these professionals must deliver value to the organization built upon one or more of the nine areas of expertise.

Raymond Noe's Predictions

Raymond Noe (2005, pp .409–426) offers the following predictions in his popular textbook, *Employee Training and Development:*

- an increased use of new technologies for training delivery
- more demand for training for virtual work
- an increased emphasis on the capture and storage of intellectual capital
- the use of learning management systems (integrated with business processes) and real-time learning
- the focus of training will be on business needs and performance
- training departments will develop partnerships with outside vendors and increase outsourcing
- training and development will be viewed from a change model perspective

Noe has been an astute observer of the field for many years, so his predictions are worth noting.

ASTD's 60th Birthday

As part of ASTD's 60th birthday celebration, T&D magazine's May 2004 issue offered many reflections on the past and predictions for the future.

Bob Pike now does consulting and coaching in addition to training. Pike believes we must "deliver what is needed, not just what is requested" (McArdle & Hanson, 2004, p. 50).

Dianna Booher now focuses on working with senior executives to develop solutions for organization-wide problems, instead of working as a trainer of small groups. She is doing more one-on-one coaching of executives. Booher's writing topics have broadened to include "the whole person, not just work life" (McArdle & Hanson, 2004, p. 52).

Several other authors in this issue spoke of the need for expanding our skill set. Whether you are new to the field, or an "old pro," you should read this issue.

SOME FINAL PREDICTIONS

Norm Kamikow, editor-in-chief of *Chief Learning Officer* magazine, cited an Accenture Learning study in which a discussion group of 23 CLOs reported that they "spend most of their resources on leadership development, followed by sales training, new product training, and IT training" (2004, p. 4). The CLOs predicted this scenario will continue to be true in the future. OL consultants must be prepared to facilitate learning efforts in all four of these areas.

David Ulrich, a leading HR author, predicts, "Business organizations in the future will compete aggressively for the best talent. Successful firms will be those that are the most adept at attracting, developing, and retaining individuals with the skills, perspective, and experience necessary to drive a global business" (1997, p. 13).

In the years ahead, senior executives of organizations will be looking for high-level tacit knowledge and experience that will add to their core competencies and competitive advantage. OL consultants will be called upon to facilitate the development of these core competencies. These core competencies, in the form of highly developed human capital, will become the organization's sustainable competitive advantage.

Finally, I predict, that within the next ten years, most universities will offer an MBA course in Organizational Learning. I currently teach an Organizational Learning course in the MBA program at the University of North Carolina-Greensboro.

I believe it's a privilege to be involved in this exciting field. I would appreciate your thoughts and comments about how we can further increase our value to our clients.

REFERENCES

ASTD (2004). *Competency study mapping the future: New workplace learning and performance competencies.* Alexandria, VA: ASTD.

Beitler, M.A. (2003). *Strategic Organizational Change.* Greensboro, NC: Practitioner Press International.

Kamikow, N. (2004). Editor's letter. *Chief Learning Officer,* May.

McArdle, G. & Hanson, C.A. (2004). Same presenters, new perspectives. *T&D,* May.

Noe, R. (2005). *Employee training and development* (3rd ed). New York: McGraw-Hill/Irwin.

Ulrich, D. (1997). *Human resource champions: The next agenda for adding value and delivering results.* Boston: Harvard Business School Press.

APPENDICES
Annotated Bibliography

The purpose of this annotated bibliography is to assist you in your ongoing study of organizational learning. It is not necessary to read these materials in any particular order. Read them as part of your own learning and development plan.

I invite your suggestions for additional materials for the next edition of this book.

Communities of Practice

1. Wenger, E., McDermott, R., & Snyder, W. (2002). *Cultivating communities of practice*. Boston, MA: Harvard Business School Press.

    This is, without a doubt, the best book on communities of practice. It is written for practitioners and contains many real-world examples. The first two chapters on value and structure are extremely interesting and a pleasure to read. Chapter 3, "The Seven Principles of Cultivating Communities of Practice," is worth the cost of the book alone.

    Chapters four, five, and seven are invaluable for organizations that depend on communities of practice as a key component of their KM strategy.

2. Wenger, E. (1998). *Communities of practice: Learning, meaning, and identity*. Cambridge, UK: Cambridge University Press.

    This book is written primarily for academics. Wenger challenges educational institutions to re-think their basic assumptions about learning (e.g., its social aspects, its relationship to practice, and the role of teaching).

    I recommend his 2002 book for practitioners.

3. Lave, J. & Wenger, E. (1991). *Situated learning: Legitimate peripheral participation.* Cambridge, UK: Cambridge University Press.

In this academic book, the authors argue that most literature on learning ignores the social character of learning. The initial intention of this book was to "rescue the idea of apprenticeship." The authors studied the apprenticeships of midwives, tailors, butchers, and others. They found that learning, to a large extent, was taking place between peers, instead of coming directly from the master.

This book is more appropriate for academics than for practitioners.

Corporate Universities

Meister, J. (1998). *Corporate universities (rev. ed.).* New York: McGraw-Hill.

This is the revised and updated edition of Jeanne Meister's classic 1994 work. Countless corporate universities are based on her model. This is "must" reading if you plan to start or improve your own corporate university.

Meister emphasizes the strategic importance of the corporate university and its role as the *umbrella* for all organizational learning activities.

I highly recommend that practitioners read this book from cover to cover.

Knowledge Management

1. Davenport, T. & Prusak, L. (2000). *Working knowledge: How organizations manage what they know.* Boston, MA: Harvard Business School Press.

This is an outstanding book written by two well-respected practitioners. Davenport is the Director of the Accenture Institute for Strategic Change; Prusak is the Executive Director of the IBM Institute for Knowledge Management.

This book is full of real-world examples and practical ideas. There are valuable chapters on knowledge generation, knowledge codification, and knowledge transfer. There is also a very good chapter on the pragmatics of KM.

2. Rumizen, M. (2002). *The complete idiot's guide to knowledge management.* Indianapolis, IN: Alpha Books.

Don't let the name of this book fool you. Rumizen is a KM expert with outstanding writing skills. She discusses developing a strategic approach, building an infrastructure, dealing with change and culture, measuring and assessing, and avoiding common pitfalls.

She also includes a helpful list of books and articles in the appendix.

3. Awad, E. & Ghaziri, H. (2004). *Knowledge management.* Upper Saddle River, NJ: Pearson/Prentice-Hall.

This book is written by two academics. It provides a wide coverage of KM. The first three chapters cover the theory underlying KM practice. They go on to cover knowledge creation, capturing techniques, codification, transfer, and data mining.

At times, this book is too academic, but it is still well worth the investment of your time.

Organizational Change

1. Beitler, M. (2003). *Strategic organizational change.* Greensboro, NC: Practitioner Press International.

I am a bit biased, of course, but I believe this is essential reading for organizational learning (OL) consultants, as well as for organizational change (OC) consultants.

This book "preaches" the importance of organizational change (and everything else) being driven by the organization's strategic plan. There is a chapter on building the consultant-client relationship, a chapter on data gathering, and six chapters with step-by-step interventions for every possible diagnosis.

The major advantage of this book is its systematic approach to planning and implementing change. It's a guidebook every practitioner should keep in his or her office.

2. Kotter, J. (1996). *Leading change.* Boston: Harvard Business School Press.

This is still the best-selling book on organizational change. The strength of the book is its easy-to-read overview of the change process.

Kotter has been a faculty member at Harvard since the age of 25, so the book lacks the practical application most practitioners seek. But Kotter's conceptual overview of the change process makes this a must-read.

Kotter's eight-stage process model is detailed in chapters three through ten.

3. Bridges, W. (2003). *Managing transitions: Making the most of change* (2nd ed.). Cambridge, MA: Perseus Books.

This is great book for practitioners (managers and consultants) who are involved in the difficult work of implementing change. Bridges' work deals with the psychological and emotional aspects of change.

Bridges offers checklists and exercises throughout the book to stimulate discussion in the organization. The chapter on dealing with nonstop change is especially helpful.

In the margin of almost every page, Bridges includes quotes from great thinkers. I found the quotes to be very thought provoking.

Organizational Learning

1. Wenger, E., et al. (2001). *Harvard Business Review on organizational learning.* Boston: Harvard Business School Press.

This is a great book in the extraordinary Harvard Business Review (HBR) paperback series. The paperback series offers a collection of the best HBR articles on a variety of business subjects.

This book begins with an outstanding article on communities of practice by Wenger and Snyder. If you can't read their entire book, be sure to read this extraordinary article/chapter.

There is a chapter by Pfeffer and Sutton on the knowing-doing gap. John Seely Brown and Paul Duguid offer a chapter on knowledge transfer through casual discussion.

Perhaps the most useful chapter in the book is Hansen, Nohria, Tierney's article on managing knowledge. In this article/chapter they discuss the critical distinction between codification and personalization knowledge management systems.

Add to these chapters the work of Argyris, Mintzberg, and others, and you have a resource that every OL consultant should own.

2. Drucker, P., et al.(1998). *Harvard Business Review on knowledge management.* Boston: Harvard Business School Press.

This is another great book in the HBR paperback series. There are several outstanding article/chapters in this book; each one taken individually is worth more than the cost of the book.

The article by Argyris, "Teaching Smart People to Learn," is very helpful. Argyris explains why very smart, highly trained professionals find it difficult to learn from their mistakes and failures.

In David Garvin's article/chapter, he talks about what real people in real organizations are doing to build learning organizations. John Seely Brown discusses the importance of innovations in "how work is done" in his chapter.

Add to these, chapters by Drucker, Nonaka, and Kleiner, and you have another "must" read in the HBR paperback series.

Performance Consulting

1. Robinson, D. & Robinson, J. (Eds.) (1998). *Moving from training to performance: A practical guidebook.* Alexandria, VA: ASTD, and San Francisco: Berrett-Koehler.

The Robinsons and several of the other contributors to this edited book have made a dramatic impact on the American Society for Training & Development (ASTD). ASTD (with 70,000 members) has changed its mission from training and development (T&D) to workplace learning and performance (WL&P). "ASTD has widened the industry's focus to connect learning and performance to measurable results" *(www.astd.org)* largely because of the work of these performance consultants.

Every OL consultant, trainer, or manager should read this book to be aware of the philosophy and practice implications of performance consulting.

2. Hale, J. (1998). *The performance consultant's fieldbook: Tools and techniques for improving organizations and people.* San Francisco: Jossey-Bass/Pfeiffer.

As the subtitle indicates, Judith Hale's purpose in this book is to offer tools and techniques for performance consultants. I recommend reading this after getting an overview of performance consulting from the Robinson and Robinson (1998) book.

Process Consulting

Schein, E. (1999) *Process consultation revisited: Building a helping relationship.* Reading, MA: Addison-Wesley.

I have taught countless workshops for internal consultants and independent consultants using this book. My most frequent recommendation to practitioners is to read this classic.

This book is not only for consultants. "Everybody" says Schein, "is involved in helping relationships." This book will help immeasurably in your role as a helper. Consultants, managers, trainers, IT and HR professionals, teachers, and even police officers will benefit from learning these skills.

Read this book or take my workshop, but learn these valuable skills ASAP.

Succession Planning

Rothwell, W. (2000). *Effective succession planning: Ensuring leadership continuity and building talent from within* (2nd ed.). New York: AMACOM.

This is the best book available on succession planning. The author provides excellent guidelines on how to create, maintain, and evaluate succession planning systems.

The book is divided into four parts:
Part I - An Overview of Succession Planning (SP)
Part II - Foundations for Effective SP Programs
Part III - Assessing Key Positions & Individual Potential
Part IV - Linking SP With Other Developmental Strategies

The book contains some very helpful aids, including:
a. an interview guide for benchmarking practices
b. a worksheet to create an SP mission statement
c. outlines for training
d. descriptions of available software
e. a checklist for evaluating SP

Traditional Training & HRD

1. Blanchard, P.N. & Thacker, J.W. (2004). *Effective training: Systems, strategies, and practices* (2nd ed.). Upper Saddle River, NJ: Pearson/Prentice Hall.

Like most books on training, this book creates a somewhat distorted view of what actually goes on in corporations today. Studying traditional training alone gives the reader the impression that organizational learning is simply another word for training. Traditional training must be understood as only part of organizational learning.

This book is typically used by undergraduate college professors because of the "Exercises" and "Questions for Review" at the end of each chapter. It offers extensive endnotes but does not contain a comprehensive reference list (helpful for research or further study).

2. Noe, R.A. (2005). *Employee training and development* (3rd ed.). New York: McGraw-Hill/Irwin.

Noe's work has a broader focus than Blanchard and Thacker's. In addition to traditional training, he adds chapters on e-learning and career management.

There is brief coverage of corporate universities, virtual training, use of technology, and succession planning, but the discussions are a bit academic.

Noe's glossary is especially helpful if you are new to the field.

3. DeSimone, R., Werner, J., & Harris, D. (2002). *Human resource development* (3rd ed.). Fort Worth, TX: Harcourt College Publishers.

This book is much more comprehensive than the previous two discussed above. In addition to HRD, there are many HRM topics discussed as well.

I would recommend this book as a primer for students, but it is too academic for practitioners.

APPENDICES
Comprehensive Reference List

Ackerman, M.S. (2000). The intellectual challenge of CSCW: The gap between social requirements and technical feasibility. *Human-Computer Interaction*, 15, 179–203.

Alderfer, C. (1969). An empirical test of a new theory of human needs. *Organizational Behavior and Human Performance*, 4(2), 142–75.

Allison, W. (1993). The next generation of leaders. *Human Resource Professional*, Fall, pp.30–32.

Allport, G.W. (1937). *Personality: A psychological interpretation.* New York: Holt, Rinehart, & Winston.

Allport, G.W. (1961). *Patterns and growth in personality.* New York: Holt, Rinehart, & Winston.

American Productivity & Quality Center (1999). *Creating a knowledge-sharing culture.* Houston: APQC.

ASTD (1998). "Trends in HRD," *National HRD Executive Survey* Alexandria, VA: ASTD.

ASTD (2004). *Competency study mapping the future: New workplace learning and performance competencies.* Alexandria, VA: ASTD.

Baldwin, T. & Padgett, M. (1993). Management development: A review and commentary. In C.L. Cooper and I.T. Robertson (Eds.), *International review of industrial and organizational psychology* (Vol.8). Chichester, England: John Wiley & Sons.

Bandura, A. (1977a). Self-efficacy: Toward a unifying theory of behavioral change. *Psychological Review*, 84, 191–215.

Bandura, A. (1977b). *Social learning theory.* Upper Saddle River, NJ: Prentice Hall.

Baskett, M. (1993). *Workplace factors that enhance self-directed learning.* (Text No. 93-01-002). Montreal, Canada: Group for Interdisciplinary research on Autonomy and Training, University of Quebec at Montreal.

Beitler, M.A. (1999). Learning and development agreements with mid-career professionals. *Performance in Practice*, Fall 1999. American Society for Training & Development.

Beitler, M.A. (2000). Contract learning in organizational learning and management development. In H.B. Long & Associates (Eds.), *Practice and theory in self-directed learning.* Schaumberg, IL: Motorola University Press.

Beitler, M.A. (2000). The role of contract learning in the learning organization. *HR.com*, September, 2000.

Beitler, M.A. (2003). *Strategic Organizational Change.* Greensboro, NC: Practitioner Press International.

Beitler, M.A. & Frady, D.A. (2002). E-learning and E-support for expatriate managers. In H.B. Long & Associates, *Self-directed learning in the information age.* Schaumberg, IL: Motorola University Press.

Bellman, G. (1998). Partnership phase: Forming partnerships. In D. Robinson & J. Robinson (Eds.), *Moving from training to performance.* Alexandria, VA: ASTD, and San Francisco: Berrett-Koehler.

Bennett, J.M. (1986). Modes of cross-cultural training: Conceptualizing cross-cultural training as education. *International Journal of Intercultural Relations*, 10, 117–134.

Bhawuk, D.P.S. & Brislin, R. (1992). The measurement of intercultural sensitivity using the concepts of individualism and collectivism. *International Journal of Intercultural Relations*, 16, 413–436.

Black, J.S. & Gregersen, H.B. (1999). The right way to manage expats. *Harvard Business Review*, March-April, 53.

Blanchard, P.N. & Thacker, J.W. (2004). *Effective training: Systems, strategies, and practices* (2nd ed.). Upper Saddle River, NJ: Pearson/Prentice Hall.

Bossidy, L. & Charan, R. (2002). *Execution: The discipline of getting things done*. New York: Crown Business.

Brinkerhoff, R. (1998). Measurement phase: Evaluating effectiveness of performance improvement projects. In D. Robinson & J. Robinson (Eds.), *Moving from training to performance*. Alexandria, VA: ASTD, and San Francisco: Berrett-Koehler.

Brockett, R. & Hiemstra, R. (1991). *Self-direction in adult learning: Perspectives on theory, research, and practice*. London: Routledge.

Buckner, M. & Slavenski, L. (1994). Succession planning. In W.R. Tracey (Ed.), *Human resources management and development handbook* (2nd ed.). New York: AMACOM.

Chuprina, L. & Durr, R. (2001). Implications of foreign culture and SDL on expatriate managers at Motorola, Inc. In H.B. Long & Associates (Eds.), *Self-directed learning in the new millennium*. Schaumberg, IL: Motorola University Press.

Clark, L. & Lyness, K. (1991). Succession planning as a strategic activity at Citicorp. In L.W. Foster (Ed.), *Advances in applied business strategy* (Vol.2). Greenwich, CT: JAI Press.

Confessore, S.J. & Kops, W.J. (1998). Self-directed learning and the learning organization: Examining the connection between the individual and the learning environment. *Human Resource Development Quarterly*, 9(4), pp.365–375.

Cooperrider, D. & Srivastva, S. (1987). Appreciative inquiry in organizational life. In R. Woodman & W. Pasmore (Eds.), *Research in organizational change and development*, Vol.1. Greenwich, CT: JAI Press. (pp.129–169).

Copeland, L. & Griggs, L. (1985). *Going international.* New York: Plume.

Corporate Executive Board (1996). Building sustainable advantage: Community of practice networks. In *Heart of the enterprise: Core competencies and the renaissance of the large corporation.* Washington, DC: Corporate Executive Board, Corporate Leadership Council, pp.171–192.

Cummings T.G. & Worley, C.G. (2001). *Organization development and change* (7th ed.). Cincinnati, OH: South-Western.

Dallas, S. (1995). Rule No. 1: Don't diss the locals. *Business Week*, May 15, 117–126.

Delahaye, B.L. & Smith, H.E. (1995). The validity of the Learning Preference Assessment. *Adult Education Quarterly*, 45(3), pp.159–173.

Dixon, N.M. (1994). Organizational learning: A review of the literature with implications for HRD professionals. *Human Resource Development Quarterly*, 3(1), pp. 29–49.

Durr, R.E. (1992). An examination of readiness for self-directed learning and selected personnel variables at a large Midwestern electronics development and manufacturing corporation. (Doctoral dissertation, Florida Atlantic University.) *Dissertation Abstracts International*, A 53/06, p.1825.

Earley, P. (1987). Intercultural training for managers: A comparison of documentary and interpersonal methods. *Academy of Management Journal*, 30, 685–698.

Elliott, P. (1998). Assessment phase: Building models and defining gaps. In D. Robinson & J. Robinson (Eds.), *Moving from training to performance.* Alexandria, VA: ASTD, and San Francisco: Berrett-Koehler.

Ellis, A. & Dryden, W. (1987). *The practice of rational-emotive therapy.* New York: Springer Publishing.

Erikson, E. (1980). *Identity and the life cycle.* New York: Norton.

Ford, J., Smith, E., Weissbein, D., Gully, S., & Salas, E. (1998). Relationships of goal orientation, metacognitive activity, and practice strategies with learning outcomes and transfer. *Journal of Applied Psychology*, 83: 218–33.

Fordyce, J.K. & Weil, R. (1971). *Managing with people.* Reading, MA: Addison-Wesley.

Foucher, R. (1995). *Enhancing self-directed learning in the workplace: A model and a research agenda.* (Text No. 95-01-005). Montreal, Canada: Group for Interdisciplinary Research on Autonomy and Training, University of Quebec at Montreal.

Garrison, D.R. (1987). Self-directed and distance learning: Facilitating self-directed learning beyond the institutional setting. *International Journal of Lifelong Education*, 6(4), pp. 309–318.

Gilbert, T.F. (1978). *Human competence: Engineering worthy performance.* New York: McGraw-Hill.

Gould, R. (1978). *Transformations: Growth and change in adult life.* New York: Simon & Schuster.

Gratton, L. & Syrett, M. (1990). Heirs apparent: Succession strategies for the future. *Personnel Management*, 22, 1, pp. 34–38.

Guglielmino, L.M. (1978). Development of the Self-Directed Learning Readiness Scale (Doctoral dissertation, University of Georgia, 1977). *Dissertation Abstracts International*, 1978, 38, 6467A.

Guglielmino, L.M. (1997). Reliability and validity of the Self-Directed Learning Readiness Scale and the Learning Preference Assessment. In H.B. Long & Associates, *Expanding horizons in self-directed learning* (pp. 209–222). Norman, OK: College of Education, University of Oklahoma.

Guglielmino, L.M. & Guglielmino, P.J. (1991a). *Expanding your readiness for self-directed learning: A workbook for the Learning Preference Assessment.* King of Prussia, PA: Organization Design and Development.

Guglielmino, L.M. & Guglielmino, P.J. (1991b). *Learning Preference Assessment facilitator guide.* King of Prussia, PA: Organization Design and Development.

Guglielmino, P.J. & Murdick, R.G. (1997). Self-directed learning: The quiet revolution in corporate training and development. *SAM Advanced Management Journal*, Summer, pp. 10–18.

Hale, J. (1998). *The performance consultant's fieldbook.* San Francisco: Jossey-Bass/Pfeiffer.

Hall, D. & Seibert, K. (1991). Strategic management development: Linking organizational strategy, succession planning, and managerial learning. In D.H. Montross and C.J. Shinkman (Eds.), *Career development: Theory and practice.* Springfield, IL: Charles C. Thomas.

Hansen, M., Nohria, N., & Tierney, T. (2001). What's your strategy for managing knowledge? Chapter in *Harvard Business Review on Organizational Learning*. Boston, MA: Harvard Business School Publishing.

Harris, P.R. & Moran, R.T. (1991). *Managing cultural differences.* Houston, TX: Gulf Publishing.

Harrison, J.K. (1992). The individual and combined effects of behavior modeling and the cultural assimilator in cross-cultural management training. *Journal of Applied Psychology*, 77(6), 952–962.

Harrison, J.K. (1994). Developing successful expatriate managers: A framework for the structural design and strategic alignment of cross-cultural training programs. *Human Resource Planning*, September, v.17, n.3, 17–36.

Hergenhahn, B.R. (1990). *Theories of personality* (3rd ed.). Englewood Cliffs, NJ: Prentice Hall.

Hinrichs, J. & Hollenbeck, G. (1990). Leadership development. In K.W. Wexley (Ed.), *Developing human resources* (Vol.5). Washington, DC: Bureau of National Affairs.

Hofstede, G. (1980). *Culture's consequences.* Beverly Hills, CA: Sage Publications.

Hofstede, G. (1993). Cultural constraints in management theories. *Academy of Management Executive,* 7(1), 81–94.

Hogan, G.W. & Goodson, J.R. (1990). The key to expatriate success. *Training & Development Journal,* January, 50–53.

Jordan, J. & Cartwright, S. (1998). Selecting expatriate managers: Key traits and competencies. *Leadership & Organizational Development Journal,* March-April, vol.19, 89–97.

Kamikow, N. (2004). Editor's letter. *Chief Learning Officer,* May.

Kelley, C. & Meyers, J.E. (1992). *The cross-cultural adaptability inventory.* Yarmouth, ME: Intercultural Press.

Kluckhohn, F. & Strodtbeck, F.L. (1961). *Variations in value orientations.* Evanston, IL: Row, Peterson.

Knowles, M.S. (1975). *Self-directed learning: A guide for learners and teachers.* Chicago: Follett.

Knowles, M.S. (1986). *Using contract learning.* San Francisco: Jossey-Bass.

Knowles, M.S. (1990). *The adult learner: A neglected species* (4th ed.). Houston: Gulf Publishing.

Kramer, D. (1990). Executive succession and development systems: A practical approach. In M. London, E.S. Bassman, & J.P. Fernandez (Eds.), *Human resource forecasting and strategy development: Guidelines for analyzing and fulfilling organizational needs.* Westport, CT: Quorum Books.

Lave, J. & Wenger, E. (1991). *Situated learning*. Cambridge, UK: Cambridge University Press.

Leibman, M. & Bruer, R. (1994). Where there's a will there's a way. *Journal of Business Strategy*, 15, 2, March/April.

Levinson, D. (1978). *The seasons of a man's life*. New York: Alfred A. Knopf.

Lippitt, G. (1970). Developing life plans. *Training and Development Journal*, May, pp. 2–7.

Long, H.B. (1989). Truth unguessed and yet to be discovered: A professional's self-directed learning. In H.B. Long & Associates, *Self-directed learning: Emerging theory and practice* (pp. 125–135). Norman, OK: Oklahoma Research Center for Continuing, Professional, and Higher Education of the University of Oklahoma.

Long, H.B. (1990). Psychological control in self-directed learning. *International Journal of Lifelong Education*, 9(4), 331–38.

Long, H.B. (1991). Challenges in the study and practice of self-directed learning. In H. B. Long & Associates, *Self-directed learning: Consensus and conflict* (pp. 11–28). Norman, OK: Oklahoma Research Center for Continuing, Professional, and Higher Education of the University of Oklahoma.

Long, H.B. & Ageykum, S. (1988). Self-directed learning: Assessment and validation. In H.B. Long & Associates, *Self-directed learning: Application and theory* (pp. 253–266). Athens, GA: Adult Education Department, University of Georgia.

Long, H.B. & Morris, S. (1995). Self-directed learning in business and industry: A review of the literature 1983–1993. In H.B. Long & Associates (Eds.), *New dimensions in self-directed learning*. Norman, OK: College of Education, University of Oklahoma.

Maslow, A.H. (1954). *Motivation and personality*. New York: Harper & Row.

McArdle, G. & Hanson, C.A. (2004). Same presenters, new perspectives. *T&D*, May.

McCauley, C., Eastman, L., & Ohlott, P. (1995). Linking management selection and development through stretch assignments. *Human Resource Management*, 34, 1, Winter.

McCune, S.K. (1989). A meta-analytic study of adult self-direction in learning: A review of the research from 1977 to 1987 (Doctoral dissertation, Texas A&M University, 1988). *Dissertation Abstracts International*, 1989, 49, 3237.

McCune, S.K., Guglielmino, L.M., & Garcia, G. (1990). Adult self-direction in learning: A preliminary meta-analytic investigation of research using the Self-Directed Learning Readiness Scale. In H.B. Long & Associates, *Advances in self-directed learning research* (pp. 145–156). Norman, OK: Oklahoma Research Center for Continuing, Professional, and Higher Education of the University of Oklahoma.

McDermott, R. (1999). Learning across teams: How to build communities of practice in team organizations. *Knowledge Management Review*, May-June, 8, 32–38.

Meister, J.C. (1998). *Corporate Universities*, (rev. ed.). New York: McGraw-Hill.

Mendenhall, M. & Oddou, G. (1985). The dimensions of expatriate acculturation: A review. *Academy of Management Review*, 10(1), 39–47.

Merriam, S.B. (1993). An update on adult learning theory. *New Directions for Adult and Continuing Education*, Spring, No. 57. San Francisco: Jossey-Bass.

Merriam, S.B. & Brockett, R. (1997). *The profession and practice of adult education*. San Francisco: Jossey-Bass.

Miesel, J.A. (1991). *A phenomenological exploration of the experience of voluntarily changing one's career during midlife. Unpublished doctoral dissertation.* The Union Institute, Cincinnati, OH.

Muchinsky, P.M. (2002). *Psychology applied to work* (7th ed.). Belmont, CA: Wadsworth/Thomson Learning.

Noe, R.A. (2005). *Employee training and development* (3rd ed.). New York: McGraw-Hill Irwin.

Nonaka, I. (1991). The knowledge creating company. *Harvard Business Review*, 69, 96–104, November-December.

Nonaka, I. & Takeuchi, H. (1995). *The knowledge creating company*. Oxford, UK: Oxford University Press.

Oechsler, W.A. (1999). Global management and local systems of employment relations. In J. Engelhard & W. A. Oechsler (Eds.), *Internationales Management*. Wiesbaden, Germany: Gabler.

Piaget, J. (1954). *The construction of reality in the child*. New York: Basic Books.

Piskurich, G.M. (1993). *Self-directed learning*. San Francisco: Jossey-Bass.

Robb, J. (1998). The job of a performance consultant. In D. Robinson & J. Robinson (Eds.), *Moving from training to performance*. Alexandria, VA: ASTD, and San Francisco: Berrett-Koehler.

Robinson, D.G. & Robinson, J.C. (1998). A focus on performance: What is it? In D. Robinson & J. Robinson (Eds.), *Moving from training to performance*. Alexandria, VA: ASTD, and San Francisco: Berrett-Koehler.

Rothwell, W. (2000). *Effective succession planning: Ensuring leadership continuity and building talent from within* (2nd ed.). New York: AMACOM.

Schein, E.H. (1987). Individuals and careers. In J.W. Lorsch (Ed.), *Handbook of organizational behavior*. Englewood Cliffs, NJ: Prentice-Hall.

Schein, E.H. (1999). Process consultation revisited: *Building the helping relationship*. Reading, MA: Addison-Wesley.

Schlossberg, N. (1987). Taking the mystery out of age. *Psychology Today*, 21(5), pp. 74–85.

Seely-Brown, J. & Duguid, P. (2001). Balancing act: How to capture knowledge without killing it. Chapter in *Harvard Business Review on Organizational Learning*. Boston, MA: Harvard Business School Publishing.

Senge, P.M. (1990). *The fifth discipline: The art and practice of the learning organization*. New York: Doubleday.

Skinner, B.F. (1971). *Beyond freedom and dignity*. New York: Bantam/Vintage.

Stolovitch, H. & Keeps, E. (1998). Implementation phase: Performance improvement interventions. In D. Robinson & J. Robinson (Eds.), *Moving from training to performance*. Alexandria, VA: ASTD, and San Francisco: Berrett-Koehler.

Tichy, N.M. (2004). No ordinary boot camp. Chapter in *Harvard Business Review on Developing Leaders*. Boston, MA: Harvard Business School Publishing.

Tough, A. (1979). *The adult's learning projects* (2nd ed.). Toronto: Ontario Institute for Studies in Education.

Trompenaars, F. (1998). *Riding the waves of culture: Understanding diversity in global business* (2nd ed.). New York: McGraw-Hill.

Tung, R. (1981). Selection and training of personnel for overseas assignments. *Columbia Journal of World Business*, Spring, 68–78.

Ulrich, D. (1997). *Human resource champions: The next agenda for adding value and delivering results*. Boston: Harvard Business School Press.

Vroom, V. (1964). *Work and motivation*. New York: Wiley.

Watkins, K. & Marsick, V. (1993). *Sculpting the learning organization: Lessons in the art and science of systematic change*. San Francisco: Jossey-Bass.

Wenger, E. (1998). *Communities of practice: Learning, meaning, and identity.* Cambridge, UK: Cambridge University Press.

Wenger, E., McDermott, R., & Snyder, W.M. (2002). *Cultivating communities of practice.* Boston: Harvard Business School Publishing.

Wenger, E. & Snyder, W.M. (2001). Communities of practice: The organizational frontier. Chapter in *Harvard Business Review on Organizational Learning.* Boston, MA: Harvard Business School Publishing.

Whetten, D. (2000). What matters most. *Academy of Management Journal,* 26, 2, p. 176.

Zemke, R. (1999). Why organizations still aren't learning. *Training,* September.

Appendices
Glossary

360-degree feedback - performance appraisal method utilizing feedback from supervisor, peers, and subordinates (may also include self-appraisal and feedback from customers)

ability - the physical or mental capacity to perform a task based upon a combination of heredity and experience

action learning - training method involving trainees working on one of their real organizational problems

adventure learning - training method utilizing structured outdoor activities

andragogy - adult learning theory; as opposed to "pedagogy" (childhood learning theory)

artifacts - visible elements of an organizational culture (e.g., furnishings, pictures, trophies, office design)

assessment centers - used for both selection and development purposes; trained assessors evaluate groups of workers while they perform a variety of exercises

association - a type of learning in which two cognitions are paired for future use

ASTD - American Society for Training & Development; a member organization of 70,000; its mission is to support workplace learning and performance

asynchronous communication - delayed communication (e.g., e-mail messages) as opposed to synchronous ("real-time") communication without delay

attitudes - a combination of beliefs (cognitive) and feelings (affect) that predispose a person to certain behaviors

attribution - process in which individuals assign causes to other peoples' behavior and their own

automaticity - the high level of skill necessary for emergency workers and those who must respond without hesitation; involves the continuous practice of the skill even after successful demonstration

baby boomers - individuals born between 1946 and 1964

balanced scorecard - measures not only financials, but other processes such as customer satisfaction and, subordinate development, among others

behavior modeling - training method that includes trainees:
a. observing a model performing a behavior
b. role playing the behavior
c. receiving feedback and reinforcement

benchmarking - process of gathering information about other companies' best practices

blended learning - a combination of online learning and face-to-face instruction

burning platform - an issue that requires change; not changing is not an option

business game - training method in which trainees gather information about a company, analyze it, and make decisions

career management - process in which employees
a. become aware of their interests and strengths
b. identify career goals
c. establish action plans
d. periodically review progress

case study method - training method in which trainees are presented with an organization's (real or fictitious) problem(s); trainees analyze the situation and make recommendations

change management - this field focuses on ways to implement change despite resistance

chief learning officer (CLO) - a senior manager responsible for promoting learning activities in the organization

classroom training - any formal training taking place away from the worksite

communities of practice - an informal group of professionals who share an interest in a common body of knowledge (a knowledge domain); see Chapter 5

competencies - skills such as facilitation skills, problem-solving skills, and coaching skills

computer-based training (CBT) - interactive training in which a computer (at home or office) provides information, asks questions, and offers feedback on trainee responses; advantages include interactivity and flexibility

contiguity - a learning theory that suggests that two objects experienced together tend to be associated with each other

contingent workforce - includes contract workers, temporary workers, independent contractors, and on-call workers

continuing education - required education for renewal of licensure for most professionals; also known as continuing professional education (CPE)

control group - a group of non-trainees (employees) that is compared with a group of trainees

corporate culture - the unspoken, shared assumptions that guide behavior in the organization

corporate yellow pages - helps employees locate others with specific expertise within the organization; may utilize individual web pages

corporate university - the "umbrella" for all organizational learning activities, including training of employees and supply chain members (e.g., suppliers, dealers, and customers)

cost-benefit analysis - a comparison of training costs to monetary and nonmonetary benefits; this process is controversial

craft guilds - associations of early master craftsmen who regulated product quality, wages, hours worked, and apprentice training

critical success factors - without these essential factors success is impossible

cross-cultural training - designed for individuals (expatriates) who will be working in foreign cultures

cross training - designed to help team members learn each others' skills

declarative knowledge - knowledge of facts and figures; as opposed to procedural knowledge or strategic knowledge

discussion method - training method that engages trainees in two-way communication; active participation is encouraged as opposed to the lecture method in which participation is not encouraged

downsizing - an organization's voluntary (although often forced by environmental factors) efforts to reduce its workforce

dual-career paths - a system that allows technical workers to pursue a technical career path or a managerial career path

EMBA - an executive MBA program designed for mature working professionals; a typical program involves face-to-face classroom meetings on Fridays and Saturdays twice per month

employee assistance program (EAP) - a company-sponsored program that provides employees confidential access to professional counseling or treatment services

equity theory - a motivation theory proposing that an individual will evaluate his or her outcomes in comparison to the outcomes of others; if inequity is perceived, the individual will change his or her behavior, thinking, or both to reduce the perceived inequity

expatriate - an individual working in a country other than his or her own native country

expectancy theory - proposes that worker perceptions are based upon three components: expectancies, instrumentality, and valence; see Chapter 2

experiential learning - training method in which trainees
a. receive conceptual knowledge and theory
b. take part in a simulation or exercise
c. analyze the activity
d. apply the theory and activity to their work

expert systems - a type of intelligent computer-assisted instruction (ICAI) that captures the knowledge and experience of experts

explicit knowledge - knowledge that can be written down or shared verbally with others; knowledge that can be codified as opposed to tacit knowledge that is difficult to capture

extensible markup language (XML) - technology used in content management; a set of rules for defining data structures and for categorizing documents

externalization - the translation of tacit knowledge into explicit knowledge

externship - an arrangement in which a company places its employee with another company for experiential learning purposes

extranet - an extension of an organization's intranet to include outside stakeholders, such as suppliers, vendors, alliance members, and customers

fidelity - the degree to which a training environment is similar to the actual work environment

force field theory - Lewin's theory that the status quo is the result of two opposing forces—driving forces and resisting forces

fundamental attribution error - the tendency to overattribute a behavior to cause within a person (e.g., effort or intelligence); one who commits this error is overlooking possible environmental causes for poor performance

Gen Xers - individuals born between 1965 and 1980

generalizing - using learning in similar but not identical situations

group dynamics - the realization that the behavior of individuals within a group may differ from their behavior when alone

groupware - electronic meeting software that enables multiple users to track and share information; multiple individuals can work on the same document at the same time

Hawthorne Effect - employees' performing at a higher level simply because they are being observed

high-potential employee - an employee who management believes has the ability to succeed at higher levels of management

human resource development (HRD) - the integrated practice of training and development, organization development, and career development

human resource management (HRM) - includes recruiting, selection, compensation, benefits, performance appraisal, and training

human resource planning - the process of identifying, analyzing, forecasting, and planning the organization's human resource needs

in-basket technique - training method involving the use of the in-basket materials on a manager's desk; trainees sort, prioritize, and respond to the materials, then receive feedback from the trainer

individualism-collectivism - Hofstede's cultural dimension indicating the degree to which people act as individuals rather than acting as a group

information overload - the concept that an individual can absorb only a limited amount of information during a given period before learning efficiency decreases

intangible assets - assets that have value to the organization, but they have no physical existence

intellectual capital - knowledge that an organization can use to generate revenue; includes ideas, different kinds of knowledge, and innovations

intelligent computer-assisted instruction (ICAI) - a computer program that can analyze a trainee's errors, then offer advice

intranet-based training - training that utilizes the internal computer network of the organization

ISO 9000 - international standards focused on the quality of the processes used in manufacturing products

job analysis - the part of needs analysis that focuses on the required KSAs of the job

job enlargement - alters a job by adding more tasks of a similar nature

job enrichment - alters a job by adding more variety, responsibility, and/or autonomy

job incumbent - the individual currently holding the job

job inventory questionnaire - questionnaire used in job analysis to identify specific tasks and responsibilities; typically given to supervisors and job incumbents

job rotation - a developmental strategy involving assignments in various departments or functions for specific periods of time

knowledge mapping - a process for identifying knowledge and skills

knowledge spiral - Nonaka's model of how tacit and explicit knowledge interact. Nonaka's four conversion processes are
a. socialization - tacit to tacit
b. externalization - tacit to explicit
c. combination - explicit to explicit
d. internalization - explicit to tacit

KSAs - knowledge, skills, and attitudes; older textbooks refer to this as knowledge, skills, and "abilities"

179

learning - a relatively permanent change in behavior, cognition, or affect

learning organization - an organization with a culture that supports continuous learning and the application of new learning

learning portal - a website that provides access to training and/or online learning communities

learning strategy -techniques learners use to organize and comprehend new material

lecture - an oral presentation by a subject matter expert (SME) to a group of trainees; its most effective use is with large audiences and for transmitting declarative knowledge

lifecycle model - suggests employees move through distinct life and career stages; and employees in the same stage are facing similar developmental challenges

local area network (LAN) - a group of computers linked by networking cables, as opposed to a wide area network (WAN) linked by leased communication lines

millennials (or nexters) - individuals born after 1980

motor skills - abilities required for coordination of physical movements

need - a deficiency state that energizes and directs behavior

needs assessment - the first of four phases in the traditional training model

offshoring - the process of moving jobs from the U.S. to foreign countries

online learning - learning with a computer with access to the internet or company's intranet

on-the-job training (OJT) - training that takes place on the job; employees are taught by fellow employees

organization development - an approach to increasing effectiveness with the use of experiential exercises based upon behavior science techniques

organizational analysis - the first step in needs assessment

outsourcing - the process of moving jobs to other domestic companies (not to be confused with "offshoring")

overlearning - involves the practice of a skill beyond demonstration of mastery; used for emergency workers or for tasks requiring automaticity

pedagogy - childhood learning theory; as opposed to "andragogy" (adult learning theory)

performance appraisal - the measurement of an employee's performance against a standard or set of criteria

performance management - goes beyond performance appraisal to include goal setting, rewards, and coaching; is an on-going process, rather than a period one

person analysis - the third step in the need assessment phase of training; follows the organizational analysis and the job analysis steps

physical fidelity - the degree to which the training program simulates the physical conditions of the workplace, including equipment and surroundings

plateau - a place in an employee's career in which future promotions are unlikely

professional development - term referring to the development needs of in-house (staff) professionals (e.g., CPAs, IT professionals, trainers, and others)

protean career - the changing and "reinventing" of today's career based upon the changing interests and values of the individual and the changing work environment

reaction evaluations - trainees' perceptions of the training content, trainers, and facilities after the training session

reengineering - a complete redesign of critical processes

reinforcement theory - a motivation theory that argues behavior is a function of consequences

repatriation - the process of expatriates' returning to their home country after foreign assignment

repurposing - the translation of a traditional training program to a Web-based program

request for proposal (RFP) - an outline potential vendors must submit to win a competitive contract

return on investment (ROI) - calculated by dividing the benefits by the cost of investment

self-assessment activities - provides employees with systematic ways to identify their capabilities and career preferences; typically includes self-study workbooks and planning workshops

self-directed learning - learning in which the employee takes responsibility for all aspects of training (needs analysis, learning design, learning documentation, and learning evaluation)

self-fulfilling prophecy - the belief that people get what they say they expect

serial discussions - message boards and chat rooms that support asynchronous communication

simulation - a training model (replica) that closely reflects the real-life situation

situational constraints - environmental constraints, such as equipment, raw materials, supplies, budgets, and time

Six Sigma - a quality-improvement process

skill-based pay - a system in which pay is based on skills rather than time on the job

social learning theory - states that people learn by observing others (models)

spaced practice - training method in which training is offered in periodic intervals

stakeholders - any person or group interested in the company's success, including owner/shareholders, customers, employees, suppliers, and the community

subject-matter expert (SME) - an individual with specialized knowledge in a particular subject

succession planning - a system for evaluating and developing high-potential employees for future advancement within the organization (often is limited to senior management positions)

survey feedback method - the systematic feedback of questionnaire (survey) responses with the intent of stimulating discussion

SWOT analysis - an analysis of the organization's internal factors (strengths and weaknesses; S&W) and external factors (opportunities and threats; O&T); the process begins with the external analysis

synchronous communication - interaction involving face-to-face discussion or real-time online discussion

tacit knowledge - knowledge that is difficult to codify; knowledge that resides in the individual

taxonomy - a hierarchy of knowledge; used to facilitate the classification and navigation through content

threaded discussion - asynchronous chat supported by a message board or chat room; replies and responses to a certain message are grouped together under the original message

traditionalists - individuals born between 1920 and 1945

training need - the difference between the required KSAs of the job and the current KSAs of the individual

train-the-trainer programs - training to prepare non-trainers, content experts (SMEs) to conduct training in the organization

transfer of training - involves the transfer of KSAs acquired during training to the job

uncertainty avoidance - an individual's preference for structured, low-risk situations

value shaping - begins with recruiting and socializing new employees into how to fit the values and culture of the organization

vicarious learning - trainee learns by observing the reinforcement (rewards) received by a model using certain behaviors

virtual expatriate - an employee assigned to a foreign country without actually being located there

virtual reality - computer-based technology that provides a three-dimensional experience

virtual team - team members separated by geographical distance, time, national culture, or organizational boundaries who work together through technology

webcasting - training provided through online, live broadcasts

whole practice - training method that covers all tasks and objectives at one time; as opposed to spaced practice

APPENDICES

Subject Index

360-degree feedback 56
360-degree performance appraisals 27

A

A-B-C model 11, 141, 142
accommodation 15
action learning 126
Active Inquiry 2, 133
adult development theories 17
adult learning theories 13
adult learning theory 104
aligning 91
alignment 25
alliances and partnerships 120, 121
andragogy 16
annotated bibliographies 53, 56
applied research 122
Appreciative Inquiry 141
apprenticeship 70
assessing 23
assessing phase 24, 137
assessment firms 81
assessment instruments 81
assessment phase 40
asset-based approach 142
assimilation 15

ASTD 2, 135, 145, 147
attitude training 27, 28
automaticity 31

B

baby boomers 90
baby-boomers 146
basket of solutions 139
BB&T University 125
behavior modeling 33, 34, 39, 85, 101
behavioralism 9
behaviorists 9, 14
Beitler and Frady Model 102
Beitler's Motivation Model 11
Bell Canada 124
Blue University 123
boot camp 126
brokering-in 139
build benches 75
business games 33
business partner 119

C

Campbell Interest and Skills Survey 27
capturing individual learning 56
career derailment 98

185

career planning 87
career planning activities 87
case studies 33, 39, 101, 105
Center for Creative Leadership 81
Central Michigan University 124
certification of the consultant 81
chatrooms 67
Chief Learning Officer 119, 145
classroom training 23
CLO 119, 145
closed-ended questions 36
coaching 85, 149
codifiable knowledge 63
codification KM 63, 64, 65, 66, 68
codified knowledge 65, 67, 70, 74
cognitive maps 15
cognitive psychology 9
cognitive reorganization 31
cognitivists 14
communication problems 26
communitarian societies 109
communities of practice 70, 72, 74, 77, 93, 146
community coordinator 75, 76
companies using SDL 51
company-specific competencies 123
competitive advantage 117, 150
competitive strategy 64, 69

compilation 32
conceptual skills 49
conducting phase 35
confrontive" inquiry 133
consultant/facilitator 4
Continuum of Business Education 49
contract learning 52
core competencies 150
corporate boot camp 126
corporate universities 73, 115, 125, 147
corporate university 116, 126
cost of training 43
cost/benefit analysis 43
counter-transference 132
critical thinking 49, 134
critical-thinking 53
Cross-Cultural Adaptability Index 84, 99, 102
cross-cultural training 87
cultural differences 106
customer/supply chain 118
customized programs 123

D

data gathering 24
debriefing 38
declarative knowledge 32, 35
diagnostic inquiry 134
direct questions 36
directory of experts 67
discussion 32, 35
discussion space 67
distance learning 46

doctor-patient model 130

E

E-counseling 103, 104
E-learning 103, 104
E-mentoring 103, 104
Eaton School of Retailing 124
electrochemical functioning 13
electronic bulletin boards 75
electronic database 64, 69
electronic databases 77
emerging practice 6
Emory University 124
employment relations 106
epigenetic principle 18
equipment simulators 33
evaluating phase 40
executive success profile 92
exemplary performers 138
expatriate manager 103
expatriate managers 84, 87, 97, 98, 100, 103
expatriate support system 104
expatriate training 146
Expectancy Theory 11
experiential exercises 86
experiential learning 53
expert model 130
explicit knowledge 64, 67, 68, 77, 146
extraversion/introversion 82
extrinsic rewards 89

F

face work 134

facilities 40, 42
FAQ files 67
FIRO Element B 27, 83
forums 67
frame-breaking 126
funding Strategy 118

G

games and simulations 33, 34, 38
gap and cause analysis 138
Gen Xers 146
general competencies 92
global business strategy 97
Global Wireless Education Consortium 124
globalization 104, 105
group exercise 38
Guglielmino & Associates 48
guidance counseling 89

H

Harley-Davidson University 122
HowTo files 67
human capital 6, 127, 150
human resource development 2, 136

I

improvisations 65
in-basket technique 33, 39
in-house consultants 3
in-house professionals 2, 79
independent consultants 3

independent learning 45
Indiana University 123
Individualism 106
Information overload 66
INSEAD 123
intact teams 83
intellectual capital 149
interactional models 17, 20
Intercultural Sensitivity Inventory 99
internal analysis 25
internal consultants 1
internal networks of experts 67
interpersonal competencies 147
interventions 5, 130, 135, 138
interviews 24
intrinsic rewards 16, 56, 89
introverted groups 37
IR University 115
ISPI 2, 135

J

job analysis 26, 40
job rotation 86, 94

K

KAI 84
key positions 92
Kirton Adaptor/Innovator Instrument 84
KM systems 63, 67, 118
knowledge management 57, 63, 77, 104
knowledge-driven economy 122

KSAs 3, 25, 27, 28, 58, 118, 138

L

lateral moves 94
leadership competencies 92
leadership development 79, 150
learning agreement 52, 55, 56, 93
learning agreements 29, 45, 52, 53, 102, 103, 146
learning contracts 52
learning goals 30
learning management systems 149
learning organization 45, 54, 58, 59
learning partners 120
Learning Preference Assessment 47
learning style preferences 14
learning-style preferences 30
lecture 32, 35, 38
lecture w/discussion 32, 35
line ownership 94
localization 106
locus of control 111
Lord Institute 121

M

management competencies 147
management development 79, 84, 86
massed practice 31
MBA course 150
mentoring 85, 93
meta-skills 51

midlife development 19
midlife transition 19
mission 117
mission statement 25
motivational theories 8
Motorola University 122
multi-company consortium 124
multinational corporations 98
Myers-Briggs Type Indicator 27, 82

N

NCBH Leadership Academy 116
needs analysis 8, 13, 56, 137
negative feedback 88
negative reinforcement 10
neuronal structure 13
new-hire orientation 126
newsgroups 67
non-training needs 24, 26, 27
non-training problems 24
nonlearning interventions 139
nonverbal cues 38
novices 74

O

observations 24
OJT 34, 40
open enrollment program 124
open-ended questions 36
Open-Source community 68
opportunity costs 99
Oracle University 115
order-taker trainer 1

organizational change 5
organizational culture 59, 65, 92
organizational results 42
outcome evaluation 41
outsourced training 120
outsourcing 149
overhead questions 36
overlearning 31

P

part training 31
particularists 109
pedagogy 16
peer to peer 70
people skills 49
people-skills 34
performance appraisal 27, 88, 98
performance appraisals 56, 93
performance consultant 2
performance consultants 137
performance consulting 2, 135, 138, 140
performance evaluation 53
performance formula 7, 24
performance improvement 145, 148
performance management systems 55, 87
performance problems 24
person analysis 27, 40
personal development 85
personalization KM 64, 66, 70
personalized KM 68
physician model 130

platform skills 35, 38, 120
position-specific competencies 93
positive reinforcement 10
power distance 106
power vacuum 131
predictions 145, 149
preference instruments 83
process 129
process consulting 2
process evaluation 41
professional competency model 147
professional development 79, 84, 88, 146
professional societies 75, 121
projected competencies 92
psychodynamics of helping 131
psychological aspects of SDL 46
psychological assessments 93
psychological conditions 33
psychological instruments 99
psychological safety 37
psychotherapy 86
punishment 10
pure inquiry 133
pure research 122

Q

questioning techniques 38

R

reaction papers 53, 56
reaction questionnaires 42
readiness for SDL 48
Readme files 67
real-time learning 93, 149
redesigning the job 28
relay questions 37
required competencies 92
reverse questions 37
reward system 10
reward systems 55, 69, 89, 90
rewards 45, 69, 88
role playing 33, 34, 39
role-playing 86
Ryerson Polytechnic University 124

S

SDL 51, 146
SDL Variables Checklist 50, 52
SDLRS 48, 84, 102
seasoned professionals 71, 74
self-actualization 8
self-awareness 81, 99
self-confidence 13
self-directed learning 45, 51, 52, 54, 119, 146
self-directed learning readiness scale 46, 84, 102
self-efficacy 13
self-organizing networks 74
self-paced modules 29
self-ratings 27
senior executive 3
sensitivity training 86
simulated cocktail party 101
simulations 101

social aspects of learning 70
social capital 70
Social Learning Theory 15, 85
social-technical gap 65
Socratic method 36
Southern Company 124
spaced practice 31
stage models 17
stakeholders 118
straddling 68
straight lecture 32
strategic business partner 140
strategic business partners 2, 145, 147
strategic knowledge 33, 68
strategic learning 5, 6
strategic management consulting 67
strategic partner 146
strategic partnering 1
strategic partners 129
strategic partnership 141
strategic plan 5, 25, 56, 63, 68, 79, 91, 117, 136
strategic planning 5, 25, 92
strategic plans 146
strategy-driven approach 4
stretch assignments 94
succession planning 90, 92, 146
surveys 24
sustainable competitive advantage 6, 45, 77, 118, 145, 150
systemic thinking 33
systems thinking 139

T

T-groups 86
tacit knowledge 64, 65, 66, 67, 68, 70, 71, 77, 146, 150
Targets for Change 5
teacher-directed 50, 51
thematic papers 53, 56
traditional trainer 137, 145, 148
traditional trainers 2
traditional training 23, 136, 138
traditional universities 121, 122
traditional university 116, 125
train-the-trainer 40
trainee anxiety 30
trainee attention 32
trainer-driven 23
training design 29, 30
training evaluation 41
training methods 32
training needs analysis 23
training objectives 24, 29
training readiness 29
training relevance 42
training vendors 120
trait models 17
transfer of knowledge 57
transfer of learning 42
transfer of training 31
transference 132
Trilogy University 126
Trilogy's boot camp 126
tuition-reimbursement 123

U

umbrella 116, 118, 120, 125, 147
uncertainty avoidance 106
universalists 109
university business schools 120
University of Michigan 123
University of North Carolina-Greensboro 150
University of Texas 125
unsupportive environment 26

V

value chain 116, 117, 121
value chain members 147
vicarious learning 15
video clip 38
videotaping 34, 86
virtual work 149
vision 25
visual learners 38

W

Whirlpool Corporation 123
workplace learning 55
workplace learning and performance 23, 145, 148
written job aids 139
written objectives 41

APPENDICES
Name Index

Allport, Gordon 17
Bandura, Albert 13, 15, 85
Beitler, David 67
Bellman, Geoffrey 137
Bennett, Chris 123
Booher, Dianna 149
Cooperrider, David 141
Drummond, Allan 126
Elliott, Paul 138
Ellis, Albert 9, 11, 142
Erikson, Erick 18
Ford, Nancy 116
Fox, Carla 125
Gilbert, Tom 138
Gilchrist, Jan 123
Guglielmino, Lucy 47
Guglielmino, Paul 46
Hale, Judith 141
Hofstede, Geert 106
Jones, Karen Neely 115
Jung, Carl 19, 82
Kamikow, Norm 150
Kirton, Michael 84
Knowles, Malcolm 16, 46, 52
Korver, Louise 115
Lave, Jean 70

Levinson, Daniel 18
Lewin, Kurt 7
Long, Huey B. 46
Maslow, Abraham 8
Meister, Jeanne 116
Muchinsky, Paul 88
Neugarten, Bernice 19
Noe, Raymond 149
Oechsler, Walter 105
Piaget, Jean 15
Pike, Bob 149
Robb, Judith 136
Rotter, Julian 111
Schein, Edgar 129
Schlossberg, Nancy 19
Schutz, Will 83
Senge, Peter 58, 74
Sprague, David 123
Thomas, Barbara 123
Tichy, Noel 125
Trompenaars, Fons 108
Ulrich, David 150
Vroom, Victor 11
Watson, John 9
Wenger, Etienne 70

About the Author

Dr. Michael Beitler (pronounced Bite-ler) began his 28-year career as a management consultant with one of the world's largest consulting firms. He has earned an international reputation as a keynote speaker, workshop leader, consultant, and author.

Michael's clients include Fortune 100 companies and mid-sized companies in manufacturing, distribution, retailing, banking, publishing, and professional services.

Dr. Beitler's teaching experience includes the MBA program of the University of North Carolina-Greensboro and the University of Mannheim's Business School (Germany's #1 ranked business school).

Mike's books and articles are used at leading universities in the U.S., Canada, and Europe (including Cornell University and the University of Michigan), and at leading corporations (including Coca-Cola and General Motors).

Please contact Michael about speaking and consulting, or with your comments and suggestions about this book, at:

Internet: www.mikebeitler.com
E-mail: mike@mikebeitler.com
Mail: P.O. Box 38353
Greensboro, NC 27438 USA
Phone: (336) 334-4534